online
AND on
mission

*Practical Web Strategy
for Breakthrough Results*

C. DAVID GAMMEL, CAE

asae & the center
for association leadership

WASHINGTON, D.C.

The authors have worked diligently to ensure that all information in this book is accurate as of the time of publication and consistent with standards of good practice in the general management community. As research and practice advance, however, standards may change. For this reason it is recommended that readers evaluate the applicability of any recommendations in light of particular situations and changing standards.

ASAE & The Center for Association Leadership
1575 I Street, NW
Washington, DC 20005-1103
Phone: (202) 626-2723; (888) 950-2723 outside the metropolitan Washington, DC area
Fax: (202) 220-6439
Email: books@asaecenter.org
We connect great ideas and great people to inspire leadership and achievement in the
  association community.

Keith C. Skillman, CAE, Vice President, Publications, ASAE & The Center for Association
  Leadership
Baron Williams, CAE, Director of Book Publishing, ASAE & The Center for Association
  Leadership

Cover design by Beth Lower, Art Director, ASAE & The Center for Association
  Leadership
Interior by Troy Scott Parker, Cimarron Design

This book is available at a special discount when ordered in bulk quantities. For information, contact the ASAE Member Service Center at (202) 371-0940.

A complete catalog of titles is available on the ASAE & The Center for Association Leadership website at www.asaecenter.org.

ISBN-13: 978-0-88034-311-4
ISBN-10: 0-88034-311-7

Printed in the United States of America.

10 9 8 7 6 5 4 3 2 1

Contents

CHAPTER 1

Breakthrough Websites

I ACHIEVED A BREAKTHROUGH RESULT WITH the very first website I helped launch. It was back in the dark ages of the web, and the site attracted thousands of visitors from around the globe and generated hundreds of inquiries for very specific services. Sounds like a huge success, right? It was a breakthrough all right—it just wasn't the one we were going for.

This site was for the Employee Relocation Council (now called Worldwide ERC) and it launched sometime in 1996, as best I can recall. I was in charge of international issues at the time and was listed as the expert contact on the website with a handy link to contact me by email. The day the site went live, I started receiving email from people all around the world with questions about how to get a visa to come to the United States. This was long before email scams were common; each of these messages was from a real person genuinely looking for help. I was blown away and knew that something new and special was happening. I have no idea how people found this page on the web with my email, but they did. The Search engine was next to useless or non-existent then, if you can imagine. The American Society of Association Executives (ASAE), as it was known then, used to maintain a single page that listed all the association websites online, to give you an idea of how sparse the web world was back then. All of these folks found me somehow through links and clicking and sharing information with others back when you had to get through some pretty significant hoops to be online.

Unfortunately, we at Worldwide ERC could not help with any of these inquiries. We didn't move people, we just talked about it. Our desired outcomes for the site were good: to support the needs of corporate relocation professionals and the experts and service providers who support them by providing some of the best information available for them in the world. We had great content and an easy-to-navigate website. We just had attracted the wrong audience. Our challenge was that people in the relocation industry largely weren't online yet. We had a mismatch between the outcomes we wanted to achieve online and the audiences that were available to us at the time. We needed a better web strategy to achieve better results online.

Fast forward a few years, and I led the launch of Worldwide ERC's first global membership body, the Center for International Assignment Management (CIAM). Members of CIAM received all their benefits via a members-only website. The site was specifically targeted at global relocation professionals anywhere in the world. Within six months, CIAM had over 1,000 members in 24 countries. This was a breakthrough result online; we provided dearly needed services and information to professionals who *wanted* to access them online in order to get their information faster and more economically than physical mail deliveries could achieve. The right audience for the outcomes we wished to achieve was online by this time, and we were able to provide tremendous value to our members. What a difference resolving that mismatch made!

Breakthrough Results: A Definition

Those experiences from my early days of working the web reinforced what I believe to be true: A website is only effective to the degree that it supports the mission of the organization it represents. Websites that create breakthrough results have a laser-like focus on achieving specific outcomes that further the organization's mission. These sites have clearly stated purposes with measurable goals. The staff managing them measure progress toward these goals and deploy content, design, and function-ality specifically tailored to further their success. The outcomes achieved online make direct contributions to the major objectives and programs of the organization, thus furthering its mission. In short, **breakthrough results online are tangible, measurable contributions to the higher-level goals of the organization.**

However, the websites of too many organizations make little if any tangible contribution to the mission, purpose, or goals they are striving to achieve. Often, these sites are the products of a committee developing a lowest common denominator solution, trying to do a bit of everything and nothing well. Other sites have grown organically over time, adding a bit here and there, leading to a similar result; dispersed effort, stale content, and poor results. These failed sites, each one a tragedy of lost opportunities, have one thing in common: no clearly formulated and implemented strategy for how the web and the rest of the online world will be used to contribute to the higher mission of the organization.

Examples of potential breakthrough results for nonprofits include outcomes such as these:

- Offering insanely easy membership recruitment and retention e-commerce processes that maximize dues revenue gathered through the site;
- Providing high-value networking opportunities for a very specific market that are unavailable at a similar caliber anywhere else online; and
- Spreading the brand message of an industry via strong word of mouth and online buzz with interactive content, media, and games.

But, as my six-year old daughter likes to preference every sentence, Guess what? Those results are only breakthroughs for your organization if they contribute value to *your* overall strategy and mission. If they don't, it's nice that you achieved those things but you are probably missing out on more valuable outcomes that you could be pursuing.

This book is about making the strategic connection between your mission and your online presence; driving your site with your top goals gives you the potential to create tremendous value via the web and internet.

Web Strategy Is the Key That Unlocks Breakthrough Results

Let's define precisely what I mean by web strategy before going any further. **A web strategy is a decision framework that enables the organization to make decisions about what content, design, and functionality will best achieve their goals.** The real purpose of this book is to give you the processes and context you need to develop a web strategy that enables you to answer those significant questions about your online presence, creating alignment between your goals as an organization and your online presence. We had great online outcomes in mind for the site we launched at Worldwide ERC in the mid-1990s. However, the audience we needed for those results was largely unavailable at that time. A properly formulated strategy would have taken that fact into account, and we would likely have pursued different goals online. Like everyone else in those early days, we were making it up as we went along. Today you have no need to take risky shots in the dark like the early web pioneers did with their sites. You can execute a practical web strategy, based on specific outcomes you need to achieve, and have an excellent chance to achieve breakthrough results.

The web strategy process I define in this book, along with the seven potential strategies for any website, will force your organization to make some hard decisions. What are our most important goals online? Where should we focus our investment in content and technology? What should we *not* do because it will not produce enough value to further our goals compared to other alternatives? That last one is often one of the most important decisions you can make. For many organizations, the simple act of deciding not to do something online is often a breakthrough result in and of itself!

Ultimately, focusing on achieving outcomes online, rather than satisfying the demands of internal constituencies, will produce a breakthrough in value. Once when I managed a web team for a large nonprofit organization, the chair of the board of ethics sent me a memo (copied to half the world) demanding a large button on the home page to click for information about ethics. I had a variety of options available to me at the time, among them:

- Ignore the memo.
- Acknowledge it and *then* ignore it.
- Form a committee to research the request and report back in six months.
- Just do what the ethics chair asked.
- Find out what prompted the memo to be sent to me in the first place and start there.

As you might guess, I went for that last option. The first two might have been career decisions, the third I found a waste of time and effort for everyone, and I didn't know if the fourth would actually solve the problem at the heart of this. So, I called the ethics chair and simply asked what had prompted the memo. She said that the board members could never find results related to ethics when they entered several key search phrases in the site's search engine. They had decided at their last meeting that placing a large button on the home page would solve this particular issue. This was a genuine problem, but the board's prescription for solving it was off base. I knew we could tune the search engine results to return anything we liked for particular searches as well as tweaking the overall algorithm to score certain phrases higher overall. Of course, the board did not know this. Why would they?

I then asked if the chair and her board would be happy if I could fix those specific searches to return the right content at the top of the results page. She said they would, so I did, and they were. This is a small example of the power of focusing on objectives. Developing and implementing web strategy that is focused on tangible outcomes will create tremendous value for your organization, your constituents, and yourself!

The other foundation for effective web strategy is audience. The outcomes you need to create online are in support of your programs, services, products, and other strategies. These outcomes then define specific audiences you must attract and serve to attain those goals. Outcomes and audiences provide the bedrock for effective web strategy. Chapter 6 goes into much more detail on the specifics of outcomes and audiences and how they interact to determine your best direction online. For now, simply keep in mind that you must attract the right people to achieve your desired outcomes online.

Top Web Issues for Executives

As I prepared to write this book I surveyed executives at a variety of nonprofit and membership organizations about their top goals and the biggest challenges they face in achieving them online. The online outcomes these leaders identified fell into three general categories: revenue, marketing, and constituent needs. Here are the most common goals mentioned in each category.

Revenue
- Increase charitable donations via the web.
- Improve sales of products and educational programs.

- Support effective membership recruitment and retention campaigns.
- Provide a platform for advertising and sponsorship opportunities.
- "More money!" as one wag, I won't identify, suggested in response.

Marketing

- Raise awareness of the value of visiting and bringing business to a specific region or city.
- Convey the full value of everything the organization does for its members.
- Convey the value of exhibiting and sponsoring meetings and events.
- Create new business leads for members of the organization.
- Strengthen the brand message of the organization.

Constituent Needs

- Support lobbying and regulatory campaigns that benefit the interests of the organization's members.
- Extend the community represented by the organization's constituents to the online world.
- Enable members to collaborate with each other online under the umbrella of the organization.

This small sample of potential outcomes shows the diversity of aims that a web presence can be used to achieve. I wrote this book to help people just like you to develop a web strategy that will be based on fulfilling the tangible results you must create as an organization.

In the same survey of executives, many respondents mentioned that their biggest challenge was cutting through the clutter of everything they do online and the full range of their programs, projects, products, and services to publish a coherent website. Sites that struggle with their own complexity, and that of the organization they represent, suffer from a lack of prioritization and discipline. The processes and ideas that I share with you in this book are intended to help you cut through that tangled web of competing priorities like a hot knife through butter. Helping my clients to distill a complex organization into a focused and effective online strategy is often cited as the most valuable contribution I make to their work and worth the full fee of the total engagement. I've piled much of that knowledge and experience into the book you are holding right now.

Process and the Seven Strategies

The heart of this book is my process for formulating and implementing web strategy. Using this process will propel you rapidly from the mission of your organization through to determining what you need to do to make it a reality online. I also offer seven strategies within that framework to identify the online approaches that will best achieve the specific types of outcomes you may be pursuing. In combination, they will give you a very good shot at realizing breakthrough results.

The process has three elements: organizational strategy formulation, web strategy formulation, and web strategy implementation. The first must be analyzed to determine what your major goals and outcomes are as an organization. The second translates those priorities into a strategy for supporting them online. The third is your plan for making it happen. Chapters 6 and 7 go into much more detail on this process.

The seven strategies fall into three categories: Revenue Strategies, Market Needs Strategies, and Marketing Strategies. The three revenue strategies explore the distinct models for creating revenue online and what that entails for your organization, technology infrastructure, and staff. The two market need strategies explore the implications of a site that is focused on serving the specific needs of a group or community online. Finally, the two marketing strategies cover macro- and micro-issues around creating demand and supporting your brand online. The three categories are covered in depth in Chapters 3 through 5. Chapter 2 provides a quick introduction to all seven and the strategy process itself.

Who Should Read This Book?

While anyone could benefit from the ideas in this book, it is targeted primarily at nonprofit organizations and the people who lead, manage, and support them. Within that broad range, here are some specific groups and the value I hope they will receive from reading the rest of the book.

Volunteer Leadership

Volunteer leaders of nonprofits are charged with translating the mission of the organization into a strategy for how they will go about achieving it. Given that, this book can provide insight into precisely how that top-level strategy can be manifested online. Depending upon the size of the organization, the board or other leadership bodies are unlikely to be involved with the direct formulation of web strategy. However, the context provided in this book can help them to understand the relationship between overall strategy and web strategy and provide useful measures for holding staff accountable for putting the web to work for their mission and goals.

Executive Directors and CEOs

I often work directly with the chief staff officers as part of my consulting projects and this book is greatly informed by those interactions. The CEO or executive director (ED) has to keep a lot of balls in the air simultaneously, managing the board and staff, all while trying to make sure goals are being accomplished. The process and strategies I define herein were strongly influenced by working closely with chief executives as we determined how they could get the most value possible from their web efforts. The content of this book will help chief staff officers to quickly cut to the chase with their staff and leadership about the specific goals they should achieve online and the best methods for doing so.

Senior Executives

The senior executives within the organization are responsible for getting things done. The book should be valuable to both the executive in charge of the website as well as other programmatic areas. Even if the web is not in your bailiwick, the strategies and processes defined here can help you and your team to work more effective with your web staff or outside providers, creating breakthrough results in the areas for which you are accountable.

Web Staff

Web staffers are often positioned, on purpose or by necessity, as servant leaders; they must lead the leaders toward using the medium and technology of the web effectively. This book should give you the tools and vocabulary to work effectively with executives in the rest of the organization on supporting their specific outcomes without necessarily implementing their desired methods. However, just because you happen to be a servant leader doesn't mean you have to be servile! Think of yourself more as Alfred, the heroic butler who was often the secret to success behind the caped crusader, Batman, and was not afraid to tell Bruce

Wayne when he was being a dolt. This book will make your job easier and your work more productive for the entire organization.

Vendors, Designers, and Technology Providers

Vendors, designers, and technology providers are critical partners in any web effort. The days of the lone webmaster doing it all are long gone. This book should help people who serve nonprofit organizations to better position the service they provide as creating valuable outcomes for their customers and clients. I've had many technology company staffers thank me for preparing my clients to work with them so well, smoothing the project for everyone, and enhancing the value of their work together. Use this book to place your products and services in the context of delivering maximum value to advance the mission of your customers.

Who Should Read This Book

- Volunteer leaders
- CEOs and Executive Directors
- Senior Executives
- Web Staff
- Technology Vendors, Service Providers, Consultants and Designers
- You!

KEY POINTS ───────────────────

- *Breakthrough Results:* tangible, measurable, contributions to the higher-level goals of the organization.
- *Web Strategy:* A decision framework that enables the organization to make decisions about what content, design, and functionality will best achieve their goals.

CHAPTER 2

The Seven Strategies

IN THE FILM *SEVEN SAMURAI,* directed by legendary filmmaker Akira Kurosawa, a village recruits a wandering samurai warrior to protect them from a hostile gang of bandits who constantly steal their food and threaten the village. The samurai recruits six more warriors to form a team of seven with which to protect the villagers. Each samurai brings his own strengths and weaknesses to the village but in concert they are a powerful force that repels the bandits.

The same is true for the seven web strategies that I have identified for nonprofit websites, although hopefully without as much swordplay! The best websites have one of these strategies as the leader, but several of the others appear in supporting roles to help the site achieve outcomes that advance the organization's mission and serve its constituents and business processes.

As you review the strategies in this chapter you will note they are each highly specific to creating tangible outcomes. This is no accident. I found early on that a focus on strategic outcomes actually tends to create results. Projects driven by technology or design but lacking a clear driving strategy tend to perform poorly, if at all. These seven strategies cover all the major ways that the website can contribute to higher-level outcomes for your organization. The strategic question then becomes, which is best aligned with your goals and which others should support that main strategy to enhance the likelihood and scope of your success online?

Every end is a means for a higher-level end. These strategic outcomes can provide significant value as the means to the ultimate ends that your organization is trying to achieve. The strategic outcomes fall into three categories: revenue, market needs, and marketing. These groupings are based on commonalities among the outcomes each strategy can generate. Let's look at the three categories and their associated strategies. Each strategy is given an initial so that we may refer to them more easily throughout the book and in your ongoing work with them.

Revenue Strategies

The three revenue strategies are very useful when the main goal of an organization's web presence is to create or channel revenue directly. Being a nonprofit does not mean that an organization cannot have revenue generation as its primary outcome for online activities! The three revenue strategies are advertising, paid content, and direct sales.

Advertising (A)

Advertising was one of the first sustainable business models for early commercial websites. Google turned advertising into a tsunami of value for publishers, advertisers, and Google shareholders. All major media websites sell advertising directly or through ad networks for a significant portion of their revenue. Some popular weblogs provide enough advertising revenue to their authors that they have made blogging a dedicated business and their sole source of income.

This same kind of advertising approach for nonprofits is somewhat less common as many organizations shy away from that kind of revenue unless it can be accrued without compromising core elements of their mission. Targeted sponsorships for specific events and programs is much more common, however, and can result in successful outcomes for nonprofit websites.

Paid Content (PC)

Paid Content as a web strategy will result in a site that provides significant value for those who have purchased access to it. The value is typically provided in a variety of content formats, including access to databases and other resources, and may even take the form of private communities where access is granted on a paid members-only basis.

Access to content may be sold as subscriptions, memberships, individual document sales, and other business models. It is a very common model for membership organization websites to allow access to the most valuable content on the site as a benefit of belonging to the organization.

Direct Sales (DS)

Websites with a direct sales strategy are those that put a premium on completing e-commerce transactions with site visitors in exchange for products and services. This is also a very well established business model in the online world, with Amazon.com being one of the most famous and innovative examples. In the context of a nonprofit organization, this strategy would result in a site that puts the sale of dues, products, event registration, and other services front and center on the site.

I have worked closely with nonprofit executives whose organizations receive over 70 percent of their total revenue via their websites. It's also not uncommon for conferences to take all of their attendee registrations online. The direct sale of products and services online is a highly relevant strategy for any organization today.

Market Need Strategies

Market need strategies are those that focus on meeting a specific need of a particular market or, more comprehensively, the overall needs of an entire market or segment. The two strategies in this category are Application or Service and Community Needs.

Application or Service (A/S)

With this strategy, the organization's focus is to provide a specific application or web-based service that meets a set of needs in its market. Many .com companies have this as their overall strategic direction. In the context of nonprofit organizations, A/S is somewhat rare as a main strategy, but is a very common supplemental strategy for promoting items such as membership directories, affinity marketing tools, and others.

Community Needs (CN)

Community needs as a web strategy will lead to a site that is focused on serving the overall needs of a particular market or market segment. Community sites, which range from traditional discussion forums to modern social networks, have this as their primary strategy. It is quite common among grassroots-driven organizations with little or no bureaucracy, such as user groups and political movements.

Many nonprofit organizations will initially think that this is their main strategy because their mission is focused on serving the needs of the community. However, after identifying the most valuable outcomes the site can contribute to the organization, it's not uncommon to decide upon other strategies to enable the site to deliver maximum value.

Marketing Strategies

Marketing strategies are designed to support the overall marketing processes and campaigns of the organization. The two strategies in this category are branding and next action.

Branding (B)

Branding as a web strategy means that the website focuses on communicating, reinforcing, and spreading the overall brand of the organization or, in some cases, is focused on a particular product or service. Sites such as this often feature rich media such as video and animation and might include viral marketing techniques.

A great example of this is the Got Milk?® television and print campaign, which also includes a website. Without looking it up, try to think of the organization behind that campaign. I've yet to meet someone outside the dairy industry who could answer that one! Their media efforts, including the website, focus purely on enhancing the brand of milk to the exclusion of all others. You can't buy the milk on the site but you can learn through interactive games what a healthy and fun beverage it is! This is an extreme example of "all brand all the time," but it's a useful illustration of branding as a key strategy for a website.

Next Action (NA)

The next action web strategy keeps the website focused on facilitating the most important next steps the organization wishes its prospects, donors, members, and other constituents to take in their overall marketing and sales/fundraising processes. When next action is used as a primary strategy, it is critical to identify which of the other strategies will serve as the best way to draw and channel website visitors into the desired actions the organization wishes them to take.

The next action strategy can be applied productively to a wide range of purposes. Many organizations use their web presence to affect the high value outcome of activating grassroots networks to contact lawmakers or regulators.

What About Social Media?

Some readers may be wondering at this point why I have not included a dedicated social media strategy among the seven. Social media includes technology and techniques such as blogs, wikis, podcasts, online video, social networking, and numerous other participatory services. These can be very powerful methods with which to achieve some outcomes but are not an end in and of themselves for nonprofit organizations.

The strategies I have chosen for this framework and process are very outcome oriented and social media may well be used in the execution of many of them, Community Needs being a prime example. Therefore, I do not isolate social media as an individual strategy but do use it as a frequent tactical element of the seven strategic outcomes.

Social media has three general elements that interact to create value: Network, Content, and Collaboration.

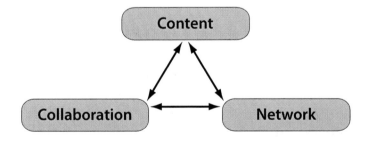

Content includes everything from blog posts to podcasts to video to links to extremely short text updates. Collaboration can include tools and systems for working together to develop content or modify and discuss existing content (think about rating and commenting upon products as an example). Network represents the tools and services that enable the distribution of content and support collaboration. When you engage in social media you are usually doing one or more of these activities, sometimes all three at the same time! Below is a table with sample outcomes for each strategy that you might pursue with social media.

STRATEGY	SAMPLE SOCIAL MEDIA OUTCOMES
Advertising	Draw an audience of value to your advertisers or sponsors by publishing content and/or supporting interaction among them.
Paid Content	Provide highly qualified and focused private social networking service for a market that values such an experience under the brand of your organization.
Direct Sales	Provide support and resources to self-forming groups of people pursuing goals and outcomes congruent with your own.
Application or Service	Enable members to include headlines from their own blog on their profile page on your site, enhancing the value of the profile and the overall membership directory.
Community Needs	Enable members or others to create their own group space on your site so they may collaborate on knowledge-sharing beyond your formal programs.
Branding	Publish a blog that constantly tells the story of your organization, the outcomes you hope to achieve, and why it matters to your constituents.
Next Action	Drive traffic to the latest news published on your site through the use of Twitter, Really Simple Syndication (RSS), and other sharing tools.

Placing the Seven Strategies into Context

How do these seven strategies relate to overall organizational strategy? What questions should they help you answer about your website execution and operation? The web strategy formulation and implementation process (illustrated in Figure 1) takes the seven strategies and ties them to the greater context of your organization, ensuring that you have the right strategies in play for your organization's desired outcomes.

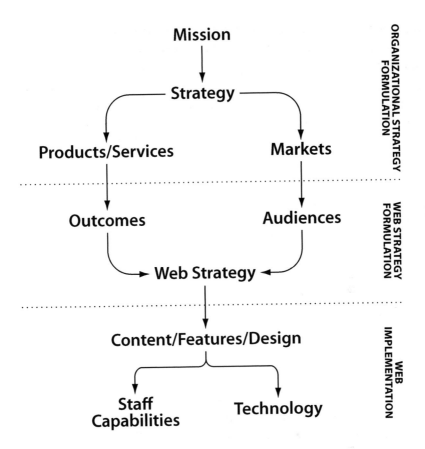

Figure 1: Web Strategy Formulation and Implementation Process

Chapter 6 will explain this in much greater depth, but let's take a quick look now at how the seven strategies play into the process of aligning your online efforts with overall organizational strategy.

Every organization has a mission or vision that it uses as a guide to the organization's purpose in this world. The mission often defines the values of the organization, which will strongly influence how it operates in pursuit of success. The board and senior leadership of the organization will then define a strategy for how they intend to go about fulfilling this purpose according to their stated values.

A good strategy will define what products and services the organization will offer and to whom they will offer them. John Zimmerman and Benjamin Tregoe, in *Top Management Strategy,* defined strategy as "the framework which guides those choices that determine the nature and direction of an organization." Tregoe and Zimmerman also introduced the concept of driving force strategy, where one strategy determines the nature and direction of the organization more than any other single factor. I have adapted this concept for web strategy, looking at how each of these seven strategies may serve as a driving force or supplemental strategy in guiding your online efforts.

Your driving force and supplemental strategies will inform what products you chose to offer and to which markets you will offer them. This information allows us to identify some specifics as to what your site should contribute to that equation. Each product and service you offer—even philanthropic endeavors—has a business process behind it. Each step in these business processes should be assessed for specific outcomes your online operations can contribute to them. These might include outcomes such as accessing further information, registering for a program or event, subscribing to a newsletter, volunteering, making a donation, and so on. Identifying these online outcomes is a key element to creating strategic alignment between your online presence and the overall goals of the organization.

How Do You Pick a Driving Force Strategy?

Answering these questions will help you to determine which strategy should be your driving force.

- Which strategy creates the outcomes that best support what we are trying to achieve as an organization? This is the really important one!

- Which strategy best addresses the audiences we must engage online? A strategy that perfectly addresses your outcomes but is antithetical to your audiences won't work.

- Which strategies are best supported by our current staff abilities and technology? This can be the decision maker when you are trying to choose between two otherwise equal candidates.

Always keep in mind that picking a driving force is statement of intent. It is a firm commitment to how you wish to achieve the overall goals set for your web presence. Picking one in which you don't yet have core strengths is fine if you have the commitment to build such strengths. That's the beauty of clear strategy: You know what you need to address to make it happen!

Website audiences are derived through analysis of your markets. Some groups within your markets are highly relevant to your online outcomes while others are not. Determining the difference is a key part of web strategy formulation. The same outcome for two different audiences may lead to dramatically different efforts based on demographic and other factors. Audiences are a significant influence upon *how* you will go about achieving your desired online outcomes. Recall the example with which I opened the book; we had reasonable outcomes that supported the mission of the organization. The audience we needed to achieve them, however, wasn't online yet! We either needed to find another audience with which we could achieve those goals or come up with alternative outcomes that we could achieve that also supported our mission.

With your outcomes and audiences in hand, you can finally begin to assess your web strategy. Figure 1 illustrates these two factors coming together to determine your web strategy. Building upon the definition of Zimmerman and Tregoe, web strategy is a framework that guides the choices about content, design, and functionality for your website and other online efforts. If your web strategy can't answer those questions, it is not a useful or relevant strategy.

The next three chapters will go through the specific characteristics of the seven web strategies, the types of outcomes each can support, and the impact that those strategies will have on your website implementation. No organization pursues all seven strategies at the same level of effort in their online presence. Attempting this usually leads to a site that does many things poorly, rather than the most important things with excellence. In Chapter 6, I will expand on the concept of a driving force strategy for your website, and will also show how you can select additional strategies from the six remaining to supplement and complement the core strategy for your site.

With your strategy determined, you are now ready to move into implementation planning, as shown at the bottom of Figure 1. The next step is to plan the content, functionality, and design that will best execute your desired strategy. A well-developed web strategy will help you make decisions about where to invest in your site and which opportunities are not relevant and should be shelved. Chapter 7 will delve into precisely how to do this.

Finally, as you proceed through implementation, the planned content, design, and functionality of your site will determine what technology is required to execute your plan, and the staff, skills, and knowledge you will need to develop or acquire. That's right; technology is one of the last things you'll talk about in this process, which is as it should be.

New Strategy, New Site?

Every organization, with rare exception, has a website today. New organizations often turn to their online presence as the first order of business once they have formed. If you are not online these days, you don't exist for a lot of people.

Given that most everyone has a website already, what does shifting, refining, or completely revamping your overall online strategy do to your site? A lot of people assume a new web strategy will require a complete redesign of their web presence. While this can be the case, it is almost always possible to make adjustments to your current site and achieve your goals without having to go through the pain, effort, and cost of a total redesign.

Complete redesigns are usually triggered by one of two things: a dramatic change in organizational strategy has occurred, or the site has been neglected for so long that it's more efficient to start over than it is to work on improving what you already have. The latter condition occurs when management fails to regularly assess and revise your web strategy. It is entirely in your control to prevent this from happening!

A good web strategy helps you to determine what content, design, and functionality you'll need to achieve your goals online. If your web strategy changes, you can compare your new needs in those categories with what you already have. You may be pleasantly surprised to realize that with a few simple additions and changes to your existing site that you can hit those new goals. Ideally, your web strategy should be constantly evolving along with your overall organizational strategy, gradually shifting your web presence over time. Changes in strategy should trigger website redesigns, not the reverse!

Conclusion

The seven web strategies cover the full range of outcomes that provide the most value to nonprofit organization websites. Like the warriors of the *Seven Samurai,* they complement each other and provide very strong solutions for a variety of scenarios when deployed in different configurations. These strategies form the basis of the rest of the book, where we will explore them in more depth individually, how they have worked for specific organizations, and how to go about formulating and implementing your own web strategy.

KEY POINTS

Definition of Web Strategy
Web strategy is a framework that determines the nature and direction of the content, functionality, and design of your website and other online efforts.

Driving Force Strategy
A driving force strategy is the one strategy that determines the nature and direction of your site more than another other.

The Seven Web Strategies

Revenue
- *Advertising*
Revenue on the site is earned by selling display advertising directly to advertisers or through a syndicated network.
- *Paid Content*
Revenue is earned by selling access to secured content not publically available on the site.
- *Direct Sales*
Products and services are sold directly to website visitors through e-commerce processes.

Market Needs
- *Service or Application*
The site provides a service or application designed to meet a specific need of your market or market segment.
- *Community Needs*
The site serves the overall needs of the community of users who visit it, often focusing on online community and social networking.

Marketing
- *Branding*
The site is used to support, enhance, and spread the brand of the organization or a specific product or service.
- *Next Action*
The site supports achieving the next action in a marketing and sales process.

Website Redesigns

Website redesign projects should be the result of a significant change in strategy, not the reverse.

CHAPTER 3

Revenue Strategies

Understanding Your Revenue

Just because you are a nonprofit organization doesn't mean that you are not highly focused on generating revenue. Healthy organizations typically have very healthy cash flow and pay great attention tending to it. The web is an increasing source or channel for revenue for organizations of all types and sizes. I have personally worked closely with executives whose organizations collect more than 70 percent of their total revenue via their website and others whose major meetings and events take close to 100 percent of their registrations online.

The key to determining how your site should support your revenue flow is to understand that flow to begin with. What products and services produce your greatest revenue overall? Which are growing the fastest? Where can the web be used to greatest effect to grow or support those revenue channels? With a good handle on where and how you make your money, you can come up with effective strategies online to support those goals.

The rest of this chapter reviews the three revenue strategies introduced in Chapter 2. These include advertising, paid content, and direct sales.

Analyzing Your Revenue

Before getting down to assessing how your online presence can best support your overall revenue, you need to know a few key details about how your organization generates cash. Here are some ideas to get you started:

- Identify the programs, services, and other revenue sources that generate a significant majority of the organization's income.
- For those revenue sources, determine what percentage currently comes in via the web vs. other sources.
- Determine the expense of receiving that revenue via e-commerce versus the mail or other methods.
- With that data in hand, discuss the following:
  - What brings in the most revenue online?
  - What brings in the least?
  - Is revenue received online more profitable?
  - Which program or service is the most amenable to online revenue collection? Which is the least?

Conducting the analysis above will help you to understand how money flows into your organization, the current role your site has in that flow, and how you may want to change that over time to increase gross revenue and total profits. This knowledge will be invaluable as you consider which of the revenue strategies in this chapter are most relevant to your goals and what you should be trying to achieve online.

Advertising (A)

Overview

Advertising revenue was one of the most common early business models for websites. The banner ad was king and eyeballs his queen. While much online commerce has gone well beyond simple display advertising, it is still a huge part of the revenue created online today. Google's Adwords program alone generated $16.4 billion in 2007.

However, is display advertising a reasonable revenue model for most nonprofit organizations? There are some organizations that generate significant revenue from online advertising sales or sponsorships. For many others, it is a minor or non-existent revenue stream. The reality for most nonprofits is that they have different drivers than traditional media websites, which lead them to approach this strategy in very different ways. Below we will consider which outcomes are best served by an advertising strategy and how that would affect the implementation of your website.

Relevant Outcomes

Which outcomes from the products and services your organization offers would best benefit from advertising revenue as an online strategy? The more common outcomes include these:

- Providing public recognition to sponsors and significant contributors;
- Promoting the products and services of the organization;
- Promoting the goods and services of your members;
- Providing enhanced value to print advertisers in the organization's publications;
- Advertising open jobs in your organization's field or industry;
- Online-only paid advertising; and
- Paid display advertising from advertising networks such as Google AdWords or DoubleClick. (Note: Ad networks are a challenging option for many organizations because of relatively low traffic and lack of control over which ads are displayed.)

Assessing the potential revenue impact for your outcomes online is critical; I can't emphasize that point enough and will probably repeat it a few more times. I've seen many organizations get lost in the weeds with an advertising strategy when it is never likely to generate significant income. I've seen one organization, though, create a focused classified advertising strategy to complement an existing print-based revenue stream and double their total gross revenue, with the new half almost all profit! The latter one shows the joy of a focused revenue strategy making the organization stronger and healthier while providing a valuable service.

A significant indicator that you have the potential for significant online advertising revenue is bringing in significant advertising or sponsorship revenue in other media and programs of your organization. If your magazines and conferences have a surfeit of sponsors, struggling to get top placement, the same is likely to be true for your site. This is because you are providing access in a new medium to the same highly valuable audience they wish to reach. If sponsorship and ad dollars are scarce throughout your organization, expecting the website to be different is probably going to disappoint you.

Audience Considerations

Your website audiences are critical for advertising strategies. Do advertisers value highly the audiences coming to your site? Are you able to sell advertising to those companies? What does your organization wish to promote to your own members and visitors? Let's consider the impact of the some of the outcomes described in the previous section.

Advertising your own products and services or promoting sponsors should be a very good fit with your existing audience. In theory, your members or other constituents already have a relationship with you through other channels, so going to your website is highly likely, thus providing the best target market for this kind of advertising. Access to your built-in audience is a key factor in why companies sponsor nonprofit organizations and purchase advertising in their publications, in addition to whatever motivations they have toward philanthropy or supporting your industry.

Other strategies can be a bit more challenging when you don't already have the audience you need coming to your site. For example, many Chambers of Commerce try to promote and drive business to their members, yet their sites might not be the first place that people in their community go to find local products and services. Advertising your members requires attracting their potential customers. You have to have a plan for attracting those audiences if you don't already have them. This is a reason why advertising revenue is typically a supplemental strategy rather than the driving force for nonprofit websites.

Advertising as a Driving Force or Supplemental Strategy?

When should advertising be a driving force strategy, where it determines the content, design, and functionality of our site more than any other? With a few exceptions, advertising is very rarely a good driving force for a nonprofit website. It is simply a poor match with the mission of most organizations; they don't exist to create profit the way media companies do by maximizing the audience of people advertisers crave to reach. When advertising is a driving force for your site, it means that your content, design and functionality will be tailored to create as many page views, by the right people, as possible. Classified advertising might possibly be an exception to this, but it is still rare that an organization exists primarily to facilitate the finding of jobs in a particular sector. If advertising or sponsorship is a significant or close to dominant revenue stream for your organization already, then this strategy may make sense as a driving force for your website. It will be much more likely to be successful online if you already have the knowledge, network, and processes for advertising sales within the organization. Absent this factor, you must be providing a unique property online, with an attendant high-value audience, in order to make advertising revenue a driving force for your site. Be sure to consider what this strategy would require in implementation and do a political gut check to be sure the organizational culture and policies would truly let you pursue it.

You may have noticed that I seem rather skeptical of using advertising as a driving force for nonprofit websites. That's because I am! I'm not ruling it out but you would need to make a very strong case for the need and will to truly carry it out successfully as a driving force. You have to be brutally honest in setting strategy. Wishful strategies tend not to lead to tangible results.

Advertising is much more commonly used as a supplement to the main driving force of the site. For many nonprofits, the audience they already serve is attractive to their advertisers and the volume of page views has little to do with it. The advertising or sponsorship sale is based on the value of the audience rather than the volume of visitors. Given this, a major criteria for using advertising as a supplemental strategy is how much your advertisers or sponsors currently spend in other areas of your organization. If it is significant, then it makes all sorts of sense to extend that activity online. If it is not high, then making advertising a strong or weak supplemental strategy online should only be done as part of a larger strategic initiative to create a new or larger total revenue stream for the organization across all channels.

Impact on Content

Content in the context of advertising often serves the same role as honey does to Pooh Bear (that I have two young daughters does impact my choice of analogy at times); it attracts the audience your advertisers wish to make an impression on.

For example, if your organization publishes an online career center where employers pay to post job listings, you might tailor your content around that application to provide value to the job seekers who are looking for positions in your industry. You might have career experts publish tips and techniques for job searching to a blog and post regular podcast interviews with major employers talking about what they look for in a candidate. Any kind of content that will maximize the right audience for your advertisers should be your focus.

In the case of sponsorships, the content becomes a bit less critical. Typically, the sponsors will be acknowledged on the home page if they are supporting the entire organization at a significant level. If the sponsor is funding a specific program or service, they are more likely to be promoted on pages related to the product or service. The content of the site doesn't have to change to attract the sponsors' desired audience, since the online sponsorship recognition is typically a secondary benefit to other exposures, such as at a conference or in a print publication.

Impact on Design

Here is where advertising discussions get interesting! How prominently should the advertising be placed in comparison to the content and services of the website? Should it sharply interrupt web visitors, such as the animated, dancing monstrosities you can see on many major media websites, or should it be subtle, understated, and close to invisible? Or somewhere in between?

Design can often become a political issue within organizations when one unit is responsible for advertising sales and another for content. There can be a tug of war between the two over how ads are positioned and displayed in your design. This is why having a clear strategy is important, it will help you to navigate these shoals and pursue a common agenda rather than seeing who has more pull and clout.

If advertising revenue is the driving force for your site, or a very strong supplemental strategy, then the ads should probably feature rather prominently in your design. If advertising or sponsorship revenue is a weak supplemental strategy, or merely an afterthought, then they should not dominate your page designs in a way that undermines the other purposes you are hoping to achieve with them.

Classifieds are an orange to these apples since these ads *are* the valuable content your visitors are coming to see. They are then displayed in the main body of the page and are often searchable as a specific application.

Web Ad Unit Guidelines

When designing your own ads or preparing to accommodate the ads of others, be sure you adhere to the standard size ads as stipulated by the Interactive Advertising Bureau (www.iab.net). This will make it easier for outside organizations to advertise with you since they should already be working with these formats. It will also help you with in-house ads because you can conform to standards built into many off-the-shelf advertisement management systems. It will also make it easier to work with outside designers or to place the same ads elsewhere on the web.

Impact on Functionality

For display advertising, you may need to provide functionality for tracking the impressions of ads running on your site, and to control what parts of the site they show up on and for how long or how many impressions they should appear. It is also not uncommon to provide reporting tools directly to your advertisers so they can see the stats themselves via a web-based application. If you sell significant display advertising on your site, then you should be able to support the level of reporting they will expect. However, this is rare for nonprofit organization websites in my experience.

It can be quite valuable to still provide those tracking tools if you run your own in-house advertisements on the site. In this case, your clients are other units in the organization and the reporting tools will help them to understand which ads perform the best for them.

Sponsorships advertising can often get by with just embedding the promotion into the page without more advanced ad tracking abilities.

Use the level of revenue you derive from advertising or sponsorships to determine how you should invest in functionality, generally scaling it up as the revenue and the importance of this strategic outcome grow. That said, many content management systems have advertising modules built in and there are also many off-the-shelf software packages to run ads on your site that don't cost a ton of money.

Impact on People

With advertising as a key strategy, what knowledge, skills, and abilities do your staff or outside providers need to successfully execute the strategy? There are several relevant areas to consider. These include:

- Marketing and sales
- Web analytics
- Design
- Content management

Marketing and Sales

If you are selling advertising directly to advertisers or sponsors, you will need personnel with expertise in forging those relationships and conveying the value of your audiences to them. This responsibility is very rarely part of the web team; it is often found in a dedicated advertising or sponsorship team or as part of the functional area that runs the sponsored service (such as meetings or publications). The person who handles online advertising marketing and sales will need to be up to speed on how to advertise effectively online in the context of your organization's website. This same skill set can be effective for in-house advertising as well.

Web Analytics

Web analytics refers to the art and science of interpreting web traffic data in order to make better decisions about how to manage your website. In the advertising context, analytics are key for measuring the return on investment for the ads you are running on your site. You want someone who can go beyond counting impressions to look at the behaviors of those viewing the ads. Are they clicking through? Do your advertisers convert a significant percentage of those who click on the ads? How much value are those ads creating for the advertiser? The more you know about the impact of your advertising, the more effectively you can price and sell it.

Design

Depending upon how you manage your advertising program, you may need some design talent for ads placed on your site. Obviously, if you run a lot of in-house advertising, then a designer can help you to come up with visually interesting display ads that attract the attention of the audience you are trying to draw. If you do not run your own ads but do place those of sponsors and advertisers, you do not need a designer for the ads themselves, but you will need some design expertise to effectively incorporate ads into your overall page templates.

Content Management

Content management is another key area for your staff managing advertising and sponsorship programs. You will often need to target ads to specific sections and pages of your site for a certain amount of time or number of impressions. Add these capabilities and responsibilities to web positions that will be tasked with supporting display advertising on your website.

Case: Advertising as Extreme Driving Force

Blogs and blog networks published by media companies provide an example of advertising as a driving force taken to its most extreme implementation. With online advertising, typically the more page views you have with the right people, the more money you will make. This creates a need to constantly publish content throughout the day that is of high interest to the people your advertisers want to be in front of. A story in the *New York Times* on June 6, 2009, gave two cases in point of this phenomenon. Two top-traffic blogs, Gawker and TechCrunch, posted unsubstantiated rumors that turned out not to be true. However, they garnered significant page views for each story. Michael Arrington of TechCrunch described it in the story as, "Getting it right is expensive. Getting it first is cheap."

The lesson here is that truly using advertising as your driving force should have a tremendous impact on the content you publish, all in pursuit of gaining more and more of the people your advertisers or sponsors want to make an impression on. In my experience, there are very few organizations that are willing to do what it takes to be successful at this strategy, which is almost always a good thing! It can be a powerful supplemental strategy but is an odd duck for a driving force in the nonprofit world.

Paid Content (PC)

Overview

The Paid Content strategy is one where a significant amount of value provided by the site is only accessible to those who have paid for it in some fashion. Models include memberships, subscriptions, day passes, and others. The basic premise is that something of value is locked away unless you pay the toll.

Paid content has fallen in and out of favor among the .com crowd over the years. As of this writing, for mainstream websites, the business model of choice is often to provide free content that is slathered with an ample helping of advertisements. There are also "freemium" models, where basic access is given to content or an application but the advanced features or full content is only given to those who pay for the access.

In the nonprofit world, paid content is a very common strategy among membership organizations. When someone joins an organization, having full access to content unavailable to the public can be a powerful way to deliver immediate value. Member-only content can also be a powerful marketing tool when positioned properly on the site. The obvious presence of such content will convey the value of what is available, which, combined with obvious leads to join in order to gain access, can drive membership recruitment. More on that in a bit.

Paid content can also be tied directly and/or exclusively to a publication. Scholarly publications, in particular, often include an online subscription, or for an additional fee, provide access online to the content in the print publication as well. This model is under some pressure for publishers, however, as the free access movement is advocating open access to science and research online.

Paid content models are not as prevalent among foundations and charities, although they may have areas of their sites that serve as a private extranet to their community and/or constituencies.

Relevant Outcomes

Not surprisingly, paid content models are often used to support outcomes related to the value of the membership or subscription. These outcomes might include

- Making evident the value of membership or subscription online;
- Delivering upon the value promise of membership or subscription;
- Prompting nonmembers to join or subscribe; and
- Generating revenue from online access.

Paid content sections of a website are often used to dramatically highlight to non-subscribers the added value of having access to the organization's resources. With this type of outcome it is imperative that those without access can clearly understand the scope and value of what is available.

Likewise, once they understand that value, there should be obvious paths to becoming a member or subscriber. The login page is a great marketing and conversation tool for those who don't have access yet in this strategic context. A login presented when a members-only resource is requested should highlight the following in order to drive membership:

- Title and description of the requested resource;
- What credentials are required to access it, such as membership or a specific subscription;
- Quick summary of total benefits of joining or subscribing; and
- A huge, unmissable button to join or subscribe.

Pretty straight forward, but a lot of organizations leave this out and never consider the missed value of people stuck at the login page.

Ultimately, the paid content must deliver value to the members or subscribers. It can be easy to forget this in the planning stages when thinking about marketing and the mechanics of offering secured access. You have to ask, how valuable is this content? Is it of value to the people we hope to serve online? How can we continue to grow and update the collection? Content is definitely king in the paid content model.

Audience Considerations

If content is king in the paid content strategy, then audience is queen. The audiences you wish to address with paid content will determine what content is of value to them and in what format. Some analysis of your overall markets is critical to correctly defining the online audience for paid content.

When looking at your overall market, consider if any particular segments of that market are more likely than others to make up your online audience for paid content. If you are a scholarly publisher, do your subscribers in academia tend to make the most of online research tools? If a membership society, are the mid-career professionals much more likely to access your website for tips, tools, and articles than the seasoned executives from which your leadership is usually drawn? Do your members typically have an assistant do their online research for them? Answering these questions will allow you to appropriately tailor your secured content for the particular audience you hope to provide value to in pursuit of your desired outcomes.

Paid Content as a Driving Force or Supplemental Strategy?

Unlike advertising and sponsorship, paid content is often used by nonprofit organizations as a driving force strategy for websites. Membership organizations gravitated to it almost immediately as websites matured beyond simple online brochures in the 1990s. For organizations whose core value is baked into membership, it makes a lot of sense to employ this strategy online. The same goes for organizations with significant subscription-based publication revenue.

However, the paid content model is predicated on the organization having a significant, renewing store of content that is of value to their members or subscribers. If your organization doesn't already have a significant source of content, then this web strategy would have to be paired with an overall organizational strategy to create such capacity and product. Without it, this may not make sense as the driving force for a website, even if you are a membership organization.

There are some interesting options available for supplemental strategy pairings if you chose paid content as a driving force. Paid content with a supplemental strategy of direct sales could lead to a site that promotes joining or subscribing online in order to gain quick access to locked-away content. Paid content paired with community needs as a supplemental strategy might develop into a site with a strong members-only community complementing a significant store of members-only content. The key in deciding how to supplement your driving force is to look for which other strategic outcomes will create synergistic effects.

Paid content can also be a good supplemental strategy when it isn't warranted as your driving force. The key is to look at how it can support your main value on the site and if you have the content and audience with which to implement it.

Impact on Content

This model has a significant impact on the content of your website. It will determine what a large chunk of it should be and how it should be provided. The key consideration for content in this model is, what content will be of the most value to our desired audience? The answer to that question will drive how you source your content and how you publish it online. The types of content can range from online copies of print publication to original content only available online. You can also have hybrids where the core of the content comes from a print source but is supplemented by additional content that can only be feasibly provided online, such as additional graphics, notes, or errata.

Another significant impact on your content is how you will provide access to it. Common models for access include Freemium, Single Tier Access, Multiple Tier Access, Variable Time Access, and Individual Document Access. Let's take at look at each of these.

Freemium access means that a very large chunk of content is freely available for all comers online but that you have an additional store of content or related services that are only available for those who pay. The free content is positioned as a way to serve a very large audience and then you focus on making revenue from the small percentage who are willing to invest in additional value.

Single tier access is probably the most common model in the association and publishing world; members get access and everyone else does not.

Multiple tier access is one where different classes of membership or subscription provide different benefits in the form of content access. It is not unusual for volunteer leaders to have access to special services for governance purposes but it is pretty rare for general content access. However, if you have a membership or subscription model that is tiered then this may be a good match for online delivery of value.

Variable time access and individual document sales are a different type of paid access that serve a person with a focused or transient need. Variable time access might include a day, week, or month-long access to paid content. Individual document sales provide access to a single document at a lower cost than buying access to the entire collection. Both of these are often used as supplements to subscription models.

In assessing how to provide your content online, you should always focus on what will best serve your audience and achieve your outcomes as part of a paid content strategy. In general, keeping it as simple as possible usually works best. If you decide to have a complicated tiered structure for access, be very sure that this is a complement to your overall organizational strategy and the needs of your market.

Impact on Design

There are several factors to consider in your design to support and strengthen a paid content strategy. Overall, the content you are providing to those with access must be very easy to use. It should be easily read on a screen and look reasonably good when printed out. Anything that impairs access to the content will impair the value you are trying to deliver online in this strategy.

Your graphic design should also highlight the fact that there is secured content available on the site. The navigation should clearly state which content is open and which is for members or subscribers only. Making paid content apparent in your navigation and overall information architecture *before* being logged in is critical for raising awareness that it's there.

Pay a lot of attention to your login page. This is a prime area for highlighting the value that users are trying to access and how to obtain that access if they don't already qualify for it. A good paid content login page should display some or all of the following:

- Title of the content the user is attempting to access;
- Short description of the content;
- A testimonial of the value of this content or the overall collection of content from an existing member or customer;
- Huge, gigantic, obvious link to sign up for an account and pay whatever is required to access the content in question; and
- Huge, gigantic button to purchase the individual piece of content in question if that is an option.

I hope you are getting the idea here that the login page is important. It is critical for growing your user base. If your login is hard to use or fails to guide traffic to ways to gain access you are leaving huge value on the table and losing people who might otherwise engage with you for a long time.

Impact on Functionality

There are three key aspects to functionality that are specific to paid content models: user rights management, user registration, and the login. User rights management is about knowing who has access to what content for how long. User registration is the process that your website visitors go through to create an account and pay for the access. The login, as you might imagine, is the process users go through to access that content.

User Rights Management

Any paid content model needs to differentiate between users who should have access to secured content and those who should not. This can get a bit complex with organizations that have tiered or other complex plans for who has access to which benefits. I'm always a fan of going with the simplest scheme possible, since it makes it easier to market and manage.

You will need to be able to define the following for each user, in order to control access:

- Login credentials, such as user name and password;
- What type of access they should have; and
- When this access expires.

Those three items will enable your site to log them in (more on that in a bit) and know what types of content they should be given access to. If you have a tiered structure for access, you will need to track each type of access for which they qualify. The last piece will tell you when to cut off that access. If they renew or pay again, your system can update that expiration date and off they go again. This kind of data often forms the core part of data integrations between content management systems and the core databases of the organization.

The other part of this is that your content management system must allow you to indicate which sections of your site and individual pieces of content should be secured for paid access. If you have multiple tiers, the system should also support defining which tier of access is allowed for each section or piece of content. These tools will be critical for your content authors and managers as they load content into the site.

User Registration

Before your members or subscribers can access the goodies, they need to have some form of login for the site. This is where user registration enters the picture. There are an infinite number of possibilities here. The key is that you keep it as simple as possible for the user. Your goal is for them to access the content immediately after they have paid.

Ideally your site will be able to immediately recognize users by an email or membership number the user provides when they register with the site and grant them immediate access. You might also want to integrate user registration for your site into e-commerce processes for membership or subscription applications, like you've seen in many retailer websites.

The thing to keep in mind as you design your systems is your ultimate goal—quickly and easily registering the user to gain access to your content once they have paid for the right to do so. Ask only for the bare minimum of data that you need in order to get them going.

Login

The login page is the gateway to your value in this model. It has to be drop dead simple. There three key functions to a login page:

- Authentication;
- Username/Password Reminder; and
- Registration.

Authentication is the process of users telling the site who they are so the site knows what they should have access to. The most common form of authentication across the web is the email address and password. I highly suggest that you adhere to this industry standard unless you have overwhelming reasons not to do so. Keep it simple and something they can remember. That's the beauty of using email addresses for the username; very few people forget their email address!

The username and password reminder feature is an essential tool on the login page. Many people forget their passwords all the time (I know I do!). Some users who do not frequent your site often will use this tool every time they want to log in. Make it simple to use, such as by providing their email address. Avoid asking for obscure data such as membership ID numbers or other bits of stuff that matter to you but no regular person is likely to retain.

Impact on People

Paid content as a strategy has a definite impact on the core skill sets your staff and outside agencies will need to provide. The key activities include

- Content Authoring and Editing;
- Content Management;
- Database Integration;
- Web Analytics; and
- Findability.

Content Authoring and Editing

Content is everything in a paid content business model. You need to provide overwhelming, powerful, insanely great content for your desired audience if you expect them to trade you money for access. The content itself may be dry as dust to a layperson but it has to be sexy stuff for your desired audience.

Therefore, you need access to lots of content on a consistent basis. Many associations will leverage their print publications to generate a lot of their online content. However, you can also post content generated as a side effect of other activities, such as conferences, trade shows, seminars, webinars, teleconferences, and others.

For example, Kevin Holland led an effort at the Air Conditioning Contractors Association to provide access to webinar content as a subscription instead of by individual purchases. The program is called ComfortU and ACCA holds at least one webinar a month, featuring the leading experts and contractors in their field. Subscribers can participate in the live events and have access to the full archive of past seminars. Their staff must be able to recruit talent, plan and host the webinar, and publish the archive. The content is often provided by their members, but is essentially "edited" by staff during pre- and post-production of the webinars.

The key elements to determine are: What content will you be adding to the site, at what frequency, and from whom will you source it? These people, on staff or not, will be your content authors. Any content going to the web for publication needs to be written, scripted, or designed to take advantage of the medium. Be sure to train and develop your content authors and editors to take best advantage of the medium.

Content Management

Paid content sites tend to have a lot of content. This means that staff who manage the site will need skills to help them organize it effectively for your users and to manage it overall. This can include tasks such as information architecture, assigning metadata (such as titles, descriptions, and keywords), determining who should access the content, or proofing the work of content editors and authors. A lot of the content managers' time will be spent on coordinating with authors, scheduling content, reviewing, and publishing content.

Database Integration

This topic is too arcane and beyond the scope of this book to go into in depth. However, the key thing to know is that paid content websites need to know who to give access to what content. The best way to do this efficiently is often to integrate it with your core database, whether that is an association management system, fundraising system, or other type of database. Often you can pull in this skill set by adding an IT person to your web team in a matrix relationship. Or, for smaller organizations, you will need to pull together your web and database providers to figure out how this will work in theory and in actual implementation.

Web Analytics

Your website users tell you a lot about themselves just by how they use the site. Web analytics is the practice of measuring this activity and making decisions based upon the evidence it provides. Key things to have your web staff focus on in this role include

- Success rate of your login page;
- Most popular content;
- Least popular content;
- Performance of new content added to the secure collection; and
- How well your login page drives people to register (and pay!) for access.

Analyzing these factors will help your staff to better understand what content is most valued, what content is being ignored, and how well your login page is letting people in and converting prospects to paid customers. You can and should determine your own measures that are relevant to how you deploy and provide access to your own content. The big idea is ask why your traffic patterns are like they are and then implement changes to your site in order to move the numbers in the direction you want them to go.

· ·

Exercise: Turn a Product or Service into a Subscription

Sometimes a shift in *how* you offer a product can have a dramatic impact on total revenue. ComfortU from ACCA is a great example. Kevin Holland reported that total revenues were up significantly when they switched from selling individual webinars to a subscription program. ACCA saw the added benefit of being much easier to market the overall program as well. This shift allows for a more comprehensive marketing effort and lessened the need to constantly hype each session. The archive also adds a tremendous value to the subscription at no extra cost to the subscriber or to ACCA for providing it.

For this exercise, identify a product, service, or event that you offer and consider how you might shift it to a subscription model. How would that impact your marketing and sales? What would that mean for how you support the program with your website, from content to design to e-commerce?

· ·

Direct Sales (DS)

Overview

The Direct Sales strategic outcome is one where you are selling products and services online through a store or other e-commerce application. For nonprofit organizations, this can cover quite a range of transactions, from selling knowledge products, to conference registrations, to charitable donations. The functionality for these activities is often provided by add-on modules to the nonprofit's core database system, although there are literally hundreds of hosted and turnkey solutions for much of it as well.

Online revenue used to be a footnote, but now I hear from many executives that their organizations bring in a vast majority of their revenue online. Direct sales is a critical strategy for many organizations. Let's explore how it can be applied to real world outcomes and what that means for how you develop and staff your site.

Relevant Outcomes

The main outcome for direct sales is relatively straightforward; taking payments in exchange for something. In the nonprofit world, this can include anything from membership dues to donations to conference registrations to product sales.

When considering online sales, always be sure to focus on your core revenue streams first and then grow from there. Moving a large existing revenue stream online can result in not only overall growth but lower expense in payment processing. Membership renewal is a great example of this. Sending two or three e-mails to a member asking them to renew online before mailing a paper invoice will speed cash flow and cost less per transaction than only accepting paper-based payments via lockbox or your own accounting department. The more online renewals the more you save. Also, people tend to expect to do business with you like this online and will be sorely disappointed if you don't support it.

Sometimes executives will rightly fear that online sales or revenue might cannibalize other revenue streams. This may be the case. However, it's usually better to cannibalize yourself rather than waiting for someone else to move in and devour your business. Try to keep the long view in mind while acknowledging the short-term pain or disruption that you'll have to work through.

If we break out the primary drivers for e-commerce today, they will look something like this for most organizations:

- Meeting customer expectations;
- Realizing cost savings in payment processing; and
- Growing overall revenue.

People today expect to be able to do business with you online. This is a very reasonable expectation and one that we all have to meet. They also tend to be trained by sites, such as Amazon, which focus on creating an excellent customer experience online. These are high expectations, but those organizations who meet them will do better with their members and other constituents.

Processing payments online, especially for cyclical payments such as membership or conference registration, can save a lot of money for nonprofits. Physical mailings continue to be more expensive every year, so a dues renewal payment online before paper invoices are sent can realize significant savings per member. Online payment processing is also typically less expensive than a bank lock box, or your staff working with paper forms and checks.

Finally, taking payments online creates the potential for significant growth. Easy online payment is a critical last step in many email and online advertising campaigns. None of that would be possible without easily converting these prospects once you have their attention. Direct sales is closely tied to marketing and effective e-commerce systems can essentially be considered a marketing tool, in that they make the value of the product or service being sold very apparent and easy to purchase once someone has decided to invest.

Audience Considerations

Audience considerations for a direct sales strategy revolve around understanding what can make the transaction feel safe, easy, and enjoyable for the customer. Do your desired purchasers tend to have significant misgivings about using credit cards online? Are they heavy online shoppers who value a quick and easy transaction? Factors such as these can be key in creating the experience online that will best support your desired outcomes—sales.

Audiences that have a high desire for safety in their transactions may benefit from one or more of the following on your e-commerce site:

- Extensive information about the product or service, including specific details about what will happen once the transaction is complete;
- Prominent displays of security certifications and safeguards, showing them you are doing everything in your power to protect their financial data; and
- Clearly identified next steps in each stage of the process, with a lifeline for help, such as live chat or a phone number.

If your audience tends to be one that is highly experienced in buying online, you may also want to provide shortcuts for speeding the purchasing process. Instant purchases, buttons to add a product to your shopping cart directly from search results and other techniques can be appropriate for that group.

If you are collecting charitable donations online you are facing a couple of issues with audiences. One, it has to be insanely easy to give you money, especially if your strategy focuses on collecting many small payments. The charitable feeling may be fleeting, and you need to move your erstwhile donor through to completion of the transactions very quickly. Two, transparency about how you are going to use the money is paramount. As I am writing this, more alleged Ponzi scheme artists appear to be revealed daily, who have destroyed a lot of wealth that was invested on behalf of (or intended for) charitable organizations. The apparent trend in giving now is much greater transparency about how the charity or foundation invests and what it then does with the money to create results. Determine what your giving audiences need to know about you for them to give comfortably and happily.

Direct Sales As a Driving Force or Supplemental Strategy?

Can direct sales be a driving force for a nonprofit website? Yes. The web is a fantastic platform for generating and completing direct sales for anything from products to event registration to charitable giving.

I know of several associations that primarily hold meetings and events, and their sites serve as their main channel for selling registration for those events. A site with a direct sales driving force strategy would highlight those events above all else and have a fantastic registration system. That system would be worthy of significant investment, since it is in support of the main revenue stream for the organization. Same thing goes for fundraising-focused sites; it is worth investing in optimizing your giving platform if the site is a primary channel for a significant chunk of your revenue.

However, direct sales can also be a significant supplemental strategy and can work synergistically with many of the six other strategies. For example, pairing community needs as a driving force with a strong supplemental strategy of direct sales can be very successful. Serving the needs of your community with content and services online will draw the audience to you because of the value your site inherently offers. This provides a very powerful marketing platform for selling additional products and services to these same visitors.

Ultimately for direct sales, determining whether it is your driving force or a supplemental strategy will help to determine what gets the highest profile emphasis on your site. Gaining clarity in this context makes it a solid business decision rather than the consensus opinion of a web committee that is not working toward a common goal.

Impact on Content

There are a couple of different types of content related to the direct sales strategy. One could be called dedicated content and the other feeder content. Dedicated content is that which directly supports the product, service, or donation that you are attempting to sell online. This can include anything from product descriptions to video demonstrations to testimonials. Feeder content is content that you use to drive people to individual products, services, or donations. It may overlap somewhat with dedicated content, but often it is content that is inherently valuable with a lead to further value in what you are selling online.

Dedicated content often gets short shrift on nonprofit websites, which is a shame because even a little bit of effort here can have a huge impact on sales. Amazon.com always recommends that their associates display product images on their sites because that often improves sales. Simply think about your own experience shopping online. The more information that is available about a product, the more comfortable you are likely to be with purchasing it.

For example, I love Heifer International's website, which features livestock you can fund for families in the developing world. You can buy anything from a bunch of chicks to a cow and make a profound difference in someone's life across the globe. Each item has pictures and detailed descriptions of how that gift will specifically help a family. This is much more powerful than simply having a prompt to donate $500.

Which is more compelling to you, buying a cow for a family that will dramatically improve their quality of life or giving $500 to a charity that supports the needy in developing countries?

Impact on Design

Similar to content, the design of a site with a direct sales strategy should focus on easing each transaction and conveying the value of the items in question. The higher the volume of the e-commerce transactions on your site, the more critical the user interface design of your shopping cart becomes. Losing 30 percent of your buyers because of a usability problem is never good, but it's criminal to leave large sums of revenue on the table when your volume of transactions is high. Likewise, the design supporting your individual product displays must convey the level of quality, authority, and security people need to feel comfortable with making the leap to invest with your organization online.

The overriding thing to keep in mind with design and direct sales—*better usability equals better revenue.*

The interface for your online store should be thoroughly tested with a representative sample of your online audiences to ensure that it is working well for them. While there are sophisticated tools and methods for conducting usability studies, simply watching a sample of people using your site to complete basic tasks can be highly edifying to observe where they stumble. Likewise, measuring your web traffic as it flows through your e-commerce system can give your web designers critical clues as to where they can make changes to improve the user experience and enhance your online revenue.

Beyond the transactional interface, the design of your site should convey the emotional value of your brand in support of your sales. Referring to Heifer International again, while the graphic design of their site as of this writing is not cutting edge, it uses imagery to perfectly convey their values and the immediate benefit that donating online will have to their cause. This applies to the overall design of your site as well as to how you structure and present individual detail pages for products and services.

Impact on Functionality

Functionality and design are closely intertwined when facilitating direct sales online. The design must present your products in the best possible light while the functionality has to be drop dead easy to use.

When evaluating systems, be sure they can support the different types of products you want to offer and the different ways in which you wish to accept payment for them.

Direct sales can have a huge impact on the required level of integration with your core data systems. Especially for membership and fundraising organizations, data about your online customers is critical for pricing and for your ongoing strategy for maximizing revenue with each person. Membership organizations often offer discounts to their members, which requires that the site knows who they are and the prices for which they qualify. Online donors must be logged and tracked so they can be contacted appropriately for further giving in the future.

The direct sales business model is a data-centric process. Make sure you are providing the data your online store needs about your customers and that your store is capturing information to enhance the quality of the records in your core databases. Finally, a top-notch web analytics package will provide the data about how visitors are using your site that your marketers and designers must have in order to make informed decisions.

Impact on People

Key skills for success in a direct sales strategy are marketing and measurement with a good helping of usability. These abilities are important to have developed in your staff and/or supplemented with outside talent. The key areas include

- Marketing and Sales;
- Usability;
- Web Analytics; and
- Database Integration.

Marketing and Sales

Seth Godin once described the web as a marketing compiler, a tool that will let you rapidly test marketing ideas without significant up-front investment. Online marketing and sales staff supporting direct sales must embody that idea. They should be well versed in split testing and email marketing, and have a solid understanding of the impact of usability on online shopping. Split testing is the practice of sending two or more variations of an email to a small subset of your list and testing which gets the better response. Split tests can be used to evaluate variations in the subject line or body of the message. If the message includes a link you wish recipients to click, then click-through rate is the key metric to compare among the different messages. Once you have a message that tests well, you can send it to your full list and maximize the response to it.

Usability

Hand-in-hand with marketing and sales is the usability skillset. This refers to knowing rules for easy-to-use e-commerce systems as well as knowing the processes, techniques, and models for testing how well your users can achieve their desired outcomes at your website. In fact, split testing, mentioned above, is in essence a usability test of your marketing!

Web Analytics

Measuring web traffic is critically important for e-commerce performance. You or your staff must know how to track your site visitors through each stage of the checkout process and see where people tend to bail out. For example, I know of one organization that discovered many members were failing to get through the login when following a link in an e-mail campaign. They removed the login step from that membership renewal process by providing a secure link in the e-mail message. This one change resulted in a six-figure revenue improvement for each email broadcast. Not too shabby! Web analytical skills will also help staff to understand where your traffic comes from and which visitors tend to buy, enabling you to tailor your site to attract more of that valuable traffic.

Database Integration

Finally, database integration is critical for transaction-heavy processes such as direct sales via e-commerce. Your IT staff and/or database vendors will need to be able to integrate these key systems to capture the purchase history of site visitors. This data is the lifeblood of any organization and it must be taken care of by your staff and technology vendors.

Case: Hearst Sells Magazine Subscriptions, Not Online Content, Thank You Very Much

The *New York Times* reported on June 1, 2009, about how Hearst Magazines focuses primarily on using the web to sell print subscriptions to their publications. While they have shuttered a few publications that were not performing well enough, their overall advertising pages (a key metric for profitability in magazines) fell 6.7 percent compared to an industry average drop of 11.7 percent. Magazines published by Hearst have websites but they do not offer all or even a majority of the print content online. They offer enough to support the brand of the magazine and convey their value and then provide prominent leads to get the full value by subscribing to the print edition.

This is rather contrarian for the publishing industry, but it does appear to be working well for Hearst now. They are outperforming their competition during one of the most challenging advertising environments in decades. Their strategy is to directly sell print subscriptions online and they have focused their efforts on just that. They have likely spent less on building out their sites and supporting infrastructure compared to businesses that tried to recreate their entire publication online.

This is a great example of a focused online strategy to achieve a highly desirable real world result. Will it work forever? Who knows! No strategy is forever as the world changes at an ever increasing pace. If this approach loses its effectiveness for Hearst in the future, I would fully expect them to forge a new direction that has a better chance of creating value for their goals.

KEY POINTS

- Revenue is a critical consideration for any website.
- Advertising revenue is rarely a driving force strategy for organizational websites.
- Advertising and Paid Content strategies will have a tremendous impact on the content you will need to publish online.
- A Direct Sales strategy requires highly efficient and easy-to-use e-commerce systems in order to be successful.

CHAPTER 4

Market Needs Strategies

THE MARKET NEEDS CATEGORY OF strategic outcomes focuses on how to best serve either narrow or broad interests of your desired audiences online. The two strategies in this category, Application or Service (A/S) and Community Needs (CN), are very common among nonprofit organizations as they work to fulfill their mission online.

The Application or Service strategy is one where you develop one or more interactive applications for your site to serve highly specific needs of your audiences. Community Needs takes a broader approach to fulfilling the needs of a complete audience or audience segment. CN tends to have a much more pervasive impact on your web presence than A/S, which tends to create a highly focused offering within a larger website. Let's explore each in more detail.

Application or Service (A/S)

Overview

The Application or Service strategy is one that focuses on serving a specific need or set of needs for your desired website audiences. It is a targeted approach that zeroes in on a defined need and supports it with some form of web-based application. In the for-profit world, many .com start-ups begin life as one of these highly focused applications.

In the nonprofit world, there is a plethora of potential needs that can be served by a dedicated online application. In membership organizations you may even have groups of members or leaders lobbying for additional functionality on the site to serve their particular needs. The key, continuing the theme of this book, is to identify when an application or service is the best path to achieving the desired higher-level outcomes the site aims to support.

Relevant Outcomes

Outcomes that can be served by an online application are as diverse as the total population of nonprofit organizations. This is as it should be since you can serve almost any need with a focused application online. Let's review some common categories that I have seen across many of the organizations I have worked and interacted with during my career.

Volunteer Management

Many nonprofit organizations use their website to serve the specialized needs of their governing body and other volunteers who help guide the organization from strategy to execution. Outcomes related to supporting this group of people can range from supporting governance work via remote collaboration, to searching for new talent to nominate for leadership positions, to providing greater insight into key organizational performance metrics. To determine if these outcomes are worthy of support via a dedicated application, look to see if they benefit almost all members of the governing body or if the needs they address are key elements of critical processes for running the organization.

Professional and Business Networking

Many membership societies support and facilitate connections among their members as a key benefit. These outcomes are often ripe for support with dedicated applications. Membership directories, allowing members to search for each other using specific criteria and then facilitating their connection, have been around since the earliest websites and are a traditional example for this sector.

Advocacy and Government Relations

Many associations and trade groups are formed in part or in whole to address the regulatory and legal interests of their members. As I write this, hundreds of organizations are geared up to influence the economic stimulus package and related efforts by government to staunch the bleeding of the economy. In these and other similar efforts, many organizations leverage grassroots networks to contact legislators and regulators to express their support or opposition for various programs. The web has become the critical tool for this kind of work.

A standard advocacy outcome that is facilitated using the web is to enable a constituent to easily contact their elected representatives and send a letter that expresses the major points recommended by their association or advocacy group. Other outcomes include gathering data about members and constituents so that custom fundraising and activation emails may be sent to them, improving response rates and overall impact. During the presidential campaign of 2008, Barack Obama's campaign website, when visited for the first time, would immediately ask for your email address and zip code. They used those two simple bits of information to build one of the most powerful and effective grassroots efforts online. Experts of either party readily acknowledge the power of the campaign's online efforts.

Application Forms

Many organization sites have complex application forms that serve as a critical entry point for some of their audiences. They have transformed paper-based forms into web-based applications that walk the user through the sometimes-complex process of providing all the required information. Ideally the forms are easy and simple to complete, but when they aren't, a tool to help mange that process can be critical. Examples of these might include complicated corporate memberships requiring lots of data about the member company, certification and credentialing processes, health care and medical society membership applications, and so on.

Specialty Search

Finally, specialty search is one where a database of information appealing to a particular niche audience is part of the value you provide. GuideStar.com's search engine of nonprofit organizations and their Form 900s is an example of such a specialty search engine. Outcomes here are to provide value to your users by giving them a tool with which to search and access a highly specialized collection of data via your site.

The above categories may give you some ideas of where to look within your organization for important outcomes that might be best served by a dedicated application online. These are not comprehensive, so be sure to consider all of your programs, services, and overall value that you provide to your audiences when assessing this strategy. If a significant amount of data is involved in achieving the outcome then you may have a good candidate for a dedicated application. Most web applications today are simply an interface to a database, giving the user tools with which to add to, modify, search, display, and analyze the contents of the database.

Audience Considerations

Audience considerations for applications largely come down to what interface and functionality will make it as easy as possible for your audience to use this tool when they need it.

When do your anticipated audiences use the web? Are they at their desks all day with discretionary time to visit your site? Are they health professionals on their feet all day with little access to computers other than working with patient data? Do they tend to use the web at night because they are unable to at work? Do they primarily use mobile devices during the day?

You get the idea. Each of these factors can have a major impact on how you build and design your application. The mobile factor is getting more important every day; as internet-enabled mobile devices are nearing ubiquity, people expect to be able to interact with you online via these itty bitty screens.

Designing for the web is never going to be boring! Change is eternal and tracking your audiences' characteristics and needs is very important to make sure you are creating services that fulfill their needs now rather than what they needed last year.

Application or Service as a Driving Force or Supplemental Strategy?

For an application to be the driving force of the organization it must be the main avenue for accessing the core value of what you do, or central to the most critical outcomes for your website. In this scenario the rest of your site becomes a support system for attracting and guiding your desire audience to your application or service and then supporting them to effectively use it.

The most important factor in determining if an application should be your driving force is if it supports the most important outcomes you want to deliver online to your desired audiences. In my experience, this is pretty rare in the nonprofit world. However, applications can be critical supporting strategies for many nonprofit websites.

As a supplemental strategy, applications can really enhance the value of your driving force strategy. For example, many membership organizations may take Community Needs (next up in this chapter) as their driving force. In these cases, an application or service for searching and networking with other members can provide tremendous value to the core strategy of the site.

The value of designating an application or service strategy as a strong supplemental or driving force strategy is that you know you should invest significantly to make that application perform optimally for your audiences, since it is a central element of how you will go about achieving your overall objectives for the site.

Impact on Content

Content related to an application or service strategy breaks into two categories, content within the application and content that supports or drives people to the application.

Content within the application might be data that the application searches, displays, or otherwise interacts with. Databases of economic data, research findings, and other types of content are examples.

Content that feeds people into the application or service can be quite varied. This can include marketing copy and articles that highlight and promote the value of the application or service. When considering content throughout the site, think about what content will best drive people to your service. The content can be positioned to draw the right audiences and then provide links to the application or it can be used to create demand for the service by highlighting the problems or opportunities it addresses for the user.

Finally, applications often have "help" documentation that must be developed and deployed online to support users. The content is often available in contextualized chunks throughout the application (such as a link to a definition for a particular term or instructions on how to complete the form currently displayed) as well as in its own collection. "Help" documents often get short changed in the planning process. Don't forget this if you have a strong application strategy for your site.

Impact on Design and Functionality

I have merged design and functionality for this strategy because they go hand-in-hand to create an effective user experience. User interface design is critical for a well functioning application. When A/S is your driving force or a strong supplemental strategy, it makes sense to invest in wireframing and prototyping applications before actually programming the applications. That allows you to test your interfaces before they are set into rather expensive-to-change code. This can take some time and effort but is well worth it to assure you are maximizing the value of the application. Once it is live, don't rest on your laurels; continue to test and enhance the application over time, adding new features to continue to build the value you provide for the specific market need you are going after.

Graphically, the design of your application should support the impression you want it to create. Studies have shown that people make a judgment about the quality of a site in less than a second. At that speed, they are not reading text or gauging usability. The only thing they can evaluate in that time is the overall look of the site. If it looks like quality, then they are likely to ascribe quality value to you it. Applications that were "designed" by software engineers often reflect that. I remember reviewing an application produced by one of the big accounting firms, and when I told the engineer presenting it that it looked like it was designed by engineers, he got a guilty look on his face. User interface design specialists are worth their weight in gold because they can enhance the perceived and actual value of the application you are trying to deliver.

The key lesson of the impact on design and functionality is that the most successful organizations invest in the *design and usability* of the interface as well as the rote build-out of the functionality. Applications with poor usability are like coffee shops whose front door only opens for 50 percent of their customers. You would not tolerate that in your coffee shop so don't do so with your online applications!

Impact on People

This strategy relies on certain competencies during the design and development of the application that then recede until you come back to revamping or improving it. Therefore, for many of these it may make sense to use outside vendors and advisors during the active phases. Other skills will make sense to build into staff competencies.

Marketing and Sales

Every major application or service should have a product manager responsible for its care and feeding. Especially for highly important apps, they must be marketed to your current and potential audiences so they know of the value. If you sell access to the service, then this will be an important competency or responsibility for staff to cover.

User Interface Design and Usability

This is one of the areas that might make sense to outsource as needed. While I think any web professional should have a solid grasp of the basics of user interface design and usability, detailed studies of prototypes and live applications can often be more effectively done by an independent expert who is not vested in the application, like staff can become through day-to-day management of the service.

The key skills here are in designing interfaces to web applications that are highly usable and visually appealing for your desired audiences. If you are outsourcing development of the application, be sure to review prior work of the firm and assess the quality of their interfaces. Chances are if their reference accounts have difficult-to-use applications that you will get the same!

Web Analytics

Measurement of web-based services and applications is critical to evaluate how much they are being used, by whom, and pinpointing any spots that might be suffering from usability problems. The owner or manager of the application should be responsible for monitoring it and using the measurement stats to improve the performance of the application.

Database Integration

Many applications created in this kind of strategy will need to access or otherwise integrate with existing data sources. For example, membership and fundraising database integration can be quite common for tracking usage and providing access to the application. This skill set can reside with your developer or the vendor who created the application. The main thing to keep in mind is that you want to hire programming staff or firms who are able to tie together all the technology necessary to achieve your desired results online.

Exercise: Supercharge the Value of Your Most Important Online Application

Identify an online application or service you already offer that, hands down, provides the greatest value to your website users. Imagine that this application is the core of the driving force strategy for your website. How would you invest in this application to dramatically increase the value it offers to your users and ultimately for your organization? Can you enhance the design? Simplify user interfaces? Develop new features? Integrate with other databases? You get the idea.

Use the list of improvements and features you brainstorm to guide future development of this application. Too often, we become stymied by the vast number of potential improvements we can make to our sites. Use this exercise to narrow your focus on one high value application and then immediately do three things to increase the value it offers to your users and creates for your organization.

Community Needs (CN)

Overview

Many nonprofit organizations form to serve the needs of a particular community, field, profession, or industry. Therefore you probably won't be surprised to learn that the Community Needs (CN) strategy is a highly relevant and popular one for nonprofit websites. The vision and mission of many professional societies explicitly stipulates that they exist to serve the needs of their community. For example, the Council on Foundations, a membership organization for philanthropic organizations, states the vision of their organization as:

> The Council's vision for the field is of a vibrant, growing and responsible philanthropic sector that advances the common good. We see ourselves as part of a broad philanthropic community that will contribute to this vision.[1]

This provides a natural anchor for using CN as a key online strategy to support the purpose of your organization. Then the question becomes

---

[1] Source: www.cof.org/council/content.cfm?ItemNumber=1569&navItemNumber=2136 on March 6, 2009.

how you can best support the needs of your community online in a way that is consistent with the purpose of your organization.

Social media, which continues to be a white-hot buzzword around the web, can often be a key contributor to this strategy. Many methods and technology from social media enhance the ability of people to connect, share stories and knowledge, and form a sense of community. It is a natural fit to this strategy. We'll discuss more about this below.

Relevant Outcomes

A Community Needs online strategy has to be closely driven by the larger outcomes you wish to create for your constituents. Your community may have a lot of needs that are simply outside the purview of what you wish to address. It's very important to keep focused on the specific needs that are relevant to your vision and mission as an organization. Otherwise you will dilute the total impact you can have by trying to be all things to all people. Let's explore some typical nonprofit outcomes and how they related to CN as a strategy.

Professional Development and Learning

Education is standard fare among many membership organizations and some charitable groups. This can involve in-person workshops and conferences as well as self-guided distance learning and interactive webinars. Applying a Community Needs strategy to these activities could result in supporting the overall learning community surrounding your diverse education efforts. This can be a highly synergistic strategy where you use the community to enhance and extend the education experience and drive people back and forth between the two.

Business Networking

Business and professional networking is a natural for a community needs strategy. If this is the outcome you wish to support with CN, then products such as enhanced directories modeled on LinkedIn with support for additional collaboration can make a lot of sense for you. There are numerous white label social networking tools and services out there that enable organizations to launch their own social media community. With a focus on supporting connections among a professional or business community, these tools can add a lot of value and fulfill a CN strategy quite effectively.

Advocacy and Regulatory Change

Many local and national political campaigns have used community-based strategies online to support their candidates and causes. Associations and charities are also rapidly exploring this space with some great results. In the context of your own online efforts, you should identify specifically what you want your community to do online and how you can facilitate those actions and outcomes. In many instances, it can make a lot of sense to use the social networking services that are already popular with your members to gain attention and then drive them to your site to take specific actions. This community strategy, paired with a next action strategy, can lead to more letters and calls to lawmakers on your behalf or even outreach to voters.

Collaboration

This is a rather broad category, but in general there are structured and unstructured collaboration possibilities online for nonprofit websites. Structured collaboration typically addresses the needs of formal groups of constituents and can include governance bodies and other volunteer activities. Unstructured collaboration refers to providing collaboration tools to your community and allowing them to form and disband groups as their needs and desires dictate. It is not uncommon to do a mix of the two, serving the needs of the leadership in their activities while also enabling rank-and-file members to initiate their own activities. There are so many free and inexpensive tools for collaboration online these days that your constituents could easily do so on their own. If you want to harness and facilitate grassroots activities and direct some of their energy into your organization, then you may want to support the unstructured model as well.

Audience Considerations

Audience is everything with the Community Needs strategy. Your intended website audiences are going to determine what universe of needs you can potentially address for them. Addressing needs they don't have is a classic error in too many sites! You have to conduct research into your user community in order to guide a CN-driven website strategy.

Factors to consider with your desired audiences in a community needs strategy include

- How they use the web;

- When they use the web;
- Their needs in the context of your organization; and
- How they currently interact with others online.

Researching these aspects of your audience will allow you to identify commonalities among them that will aid in guiding the implementation of your strategy. Keep an eye out for segments of your audiences that reveal commonalities within their group but significant differences with others. This can help to target them individually and best serve their needs, especially if they are a significant segment for the goals of your site.

I often hear from executives who are concerned about drawing their entire membership or constituency online for interactive community efforts. This may be impossible to do because it is hard to get all of your audience members to behave as you would like them to. Assess which elements of your total potential audience are most likely to use your services and balance your approach accordingly.

I spoke recently with an executive at an association for farm owners. She said that most of their members weren't online or had dial-up access at best. A challenging group to provide online services to! However, she did have a small group of members who were online and interacting with each and had even started their own Facebook group for networking. The association has engaged with them via the Facebook group, creating good will and positive outcomes with their small, wired, member segment. It is possible to create a focused strategy on a small scale if your audience characteristics dictate it.

Community Needs as a Driving Force or Supplemental Strategy?

Community Needs is a very common strategy for membership websites and is often in effect by default for many where no comprehensive strategy was developed to guide the site. Associations tend to exist to broadly serve the needs of their members and this will extend to their web presence.

Chad Houghton at the Society for Human Resource Management said this about the main goals of their web presence:

Achievement of specific goals related to revenue, membership acquisition and retention, and advocacy. These goals are met through providing a relevant, useful, and engaging experience for our members. Increased member engagement leads to advertising opportunities and ancillary product sales (books, seminars, etc.) Revenue enables the mission and advocacy-oriented work of the organization. But the starting point is providing a quality product and experience for the member. That's the number one objective and priority of our site.

You can see that some very specific high-level outcomes around product revenue, membership growth and retention, and advocacy all require significant and repeated exposure to their constituents via the website. Their strategy for creating this engagement is through deploying content, functionality, and design that facilitate the overall needs of that community, bringing them back to the site over and over again. This is a great example of how what appear to revenue or marketing outcomes can be best served by a using community needs as a driving force strategy.

In assessing your own direction online, consider if your ultimate goals require high traffic visits and a high level of engagement from your constituents. If so, then community needs as a driving force strategy may be your best path to success.

CN can also, of course, be deployed as a supporting or supplemental strategy. In the case of Society for Human Resource Management (SHRM) earlier, pairing direct sales as a driving force with community needs in support would lead to a significant difference in what is emphasized via the design and structure of the website. The same outcomes may be achieved but the choice of driving force sets the tone for your overall efforts in creating the site.

Impact on Content

The type and volume of content created and deployed in a community needs strategy will vary significantly from one organization to another. There are two sources of content, user-contributed and organization-contributed, that you should consider in your planning. User-contributed content includes anything your website users add to the site and can take the form of comments, ratings, tags, blog posts, wiki entries or edits, video or audio comments, or even syndicated content from their own sites. Organization-contributed content may be formal items such as news stories, reports, and articles often sourced from existing publications. Organizations can also contribute much of the less formal type of content, as you would get from users, contributed to the site by their staff or leadership.

Since most CN strategies will have a significant component of user-contributed content, the question often becomes, what content must the organization generate and publish for the community in order to attract the audience you want and to sustain the community of people who have already joined you online? Answering this question for your audiences will help you get off to a strong start with a new community needs orientation as well as to sustain your success in the long run.

User-contributed content on your site can often be new territory for some organizations. The most effective organizations employing this strategy for the first time assess their own culture and do development work with staff and leaders to understand this new dynamic and to make sure their existing policies and procedures aren't at cross-purposes with their goals. For example, I have seen organizations that profess a commitment from the top to engaging with members via social media, yet configure their firewall to block their staff from accessing such sites. Strange but true! The cause of this is almost always a lack of alignment throughout the organization (in particular with the IT department!) with the new direction for their online efforts.

Online media are becoming more interactive and rich by the day. Video and audio are quite common on everything from the one-woman blog to the corporate portals of major media companies. This content can be quite powerful because it engages more of our senses and provides variety and increased interest. Nonprofit organizations often have access to a fair amount of audio and video content through their other activities. Recording devices have also become so easy and inexpensive to use that capturing new content has fewer barriers than ever before.

Impact on Design

Facilitating a community online requires dedicated and highly usable functionality. The design of the site should also give your desired audience a sense that they belong, that it is a place meant for them.

The visual design of the space should resonate with your target audiences. When I worked with the Ecological Society of America (ESA) on a redesign of their site, a guiding principle for the site was that it make their members proud to be an ecologist and proud of their affiliation with ESA. This theme resulted in a design that featured members in the field (literally, in some cases!) and images of a variety of biomes from around the world. The design direction was intended to create an emotional resonance with the site, one that tells an ecologist looking at it for the first time, "This place is obviously intended for me!"

In considering design aspects for your community of users, think about what imagery will create the resonance that will best support your goals for them. Consider the environment or products or outcomes your members produce as well as pictures of them in action. Test the designs and images with your audiences and see if they have the reactions you wish to inspire.

Impact on Functionality

The functionality of the site for community needs will be very content-oriented. For staff, the content management system must make it easy to add content to the site in all forms that you wish to publish based on what will draw and sustain your desired audiences. Staff must also have adequate tools for reviewing and managing user-contributed content. For the user-contributed content, the functionality has to be drop-dead easy. Every small barrier will cost you a lot of participation. While the site may be the most important part of your job, it is rarely the case for your users. Easy-to-use sites enhance participation while hard-to-use sites have a hard time getting off the ground.

Development teams and technology vendors will provide the most appropriate functionality when given specific outcomes to achieve and metrics of what the results will look like. For example, let's say your organization wishes to facilitate collaboration among chapters spread across the country and that a lot of their work focuses on developing policy recommendations for local governments. Specifying the outcome you wish to support for these groups and how they work together gives excellent guidance and will lead to a better solution than simply stating, "our chapters need a collaboration portal."

Impact on People

The Community Needs strategy can have a big impact on staff and volunteers. Just as a large annual meeting requires a cast of hundreds to pull off, so can a comprehensive and vibrant online community. Below are the major areas of activity for staff and volunteer leaders when implementing a community needs strategy.

Content Authoring and Management

Managing content in a community needs context is even more audience-driven than most strategies. You want to provide content that will draw and sustain your community and the interactions they wish to have via your site. Therefore much of the content must be designed for creating interaction by facilitating and enabling socialization among your users. Just posting articles from your newsletter or magazine won't do it, although those certainly do provide value. Content that is meant to be shared, expanded, rated, critiqued, or otherwise *used* by your visitors can be referred to as a social object.

Staff and volunteers who support this function will need the skills and knowledge to create such content, seed it into your community, and track what tends to generate reaction and what doesn't. The basic of content management skills apply (covered earlier in the book), but also include this social element for a community needs strategy. This is not an overly difficult set of skills to train or develop. The most important aspects are to not only post the content but to monitor what gets traction and what doesn't and feed that intelligence back into the overall content development process.

Community Management/Engagement

Facilitating engagement of your website users with each other and your organization involves several types of activities by staff who manage the site. These primary activities include listening, commenting, and connecting on your own site as well as other places where your desired audiences spend their time online.

Listening means searching out where your audiences are engaging online and at least lurking in those places as well as paying attention to activity on your own websites. This is a critical base activity for community strategy implementation. The knowledge and information gleaned from listening has to be plugged back into the organization as well.

Connecting and commenting come into play after you have been listening for a while. You will begin to recognize people and themes that are related to what you are trying to achieve with your community or overall for your organization. Organizations that react proactively to comments about them online tend to be better perceived. Comcast has a team of over 10 staff whose sole job is to find complaints about them online and see how they can make it right for the customer. I refer to this as conducting customer service as a public performance. The value of the interaction is even the perception of everyone watching than that of the individual customer.

Actively connecting with people online and engaging in the conversation is the single best way to grow participation in your own community efforts. It sets the tone, draws attention, and seeds activity very effectively when done consciously as a regular process over time.

Video/Audio Production

Video and audio content are becoming more prominent in community-driven websites. The organization may produce and post the content and participants may post their own rich content as well. Meetings and events tend to generate many snippets of content in these formats if the attendees are early adopters of technology. For staff-driven efforts, someone on the team should have skills in working with basic video and audio production and techniques for posting them online with your own tools or the variety of hosting services that are available. These skills are often easily self-taught or can be picked up quickly with online tutorials. The beauty of this kind of content, as of this writing, is that relatively low production quality is usually acceptable by your audiences if the content itself is of value and interest.

Case: Center for Liberty in the Middle East

The Center for Liberty in the Middle East (CLIME) (www.mideastliberty.org) was founded as a nonprofit organization dedicated to promoting liberal democratic values in the Middle East. According to Jeff Cobb, CLIME's e-learning consultant, "CLIME has helped a number of activists in the Middle East improve their grass-roots outreach, communications and lobbying skills, and deepen their understanding of liberal democracy. Beneficiaries of CLIME training and mentoring have successfully run for public office and assumed a variety of other leadership roles within their communities."

CLIME is a good example of an online driving force strategy that serves the specific needs of their community. They put together an e-learning program and technical infrastructure that enabled them to train and educate people throughout the Middle East who supported the same outcomes as CLIME. Leveraging the web and internet to deliver the education dramatically expanded their reach without always needing staff or partners on the ground in every location. The online education effort is how CLIME has chosen to serve the needs of their community online in pursuit of their overall mission.

KEY POINTS

- An Application/Service (A/S) strategy tends to create a highly focused offering that meets a specific need with an interactive application.

- A/S strategies lead to focused investment in an individual or small set of online applications.

- Community Needs (CN) as a strategy is a very broad approach to serving the needs of a specific community or segment of your online audience.

- CN strategies can lead to a broad array of tools, services, and content being deployed online to meet the needs you wish to address.

- CN strategies can often benefit from the use of social media and other participatory technologies.

CHAPTER 5

Marketing Strategies

Yᴏᴜ ᴄᴏᴜʟᴅ ᴀʀɢᴜᴇ ᴛʜᴀᴛ ᴍᴀʀᴋᴇᴛɪɴɢ is the core of any website. As a medium, the web has certainly captured the imagination of marketers with its potential reach and immediacy with consumers and purchasers of all kinds. B2B, B2C, viral, eyeballs, and other buzzwords have all entered the lexicon via marketers exploring how to create value with the web and the internet.

Marketing with the web is a key activity for almost any nonprofit organization. For purposes of strategy, there are two approaches: supporting your overall brand or facilitating specific next actions in your conversion process. The former is a longer-term strategy while the latter tends to support tactical marketing outcomes. Let's explore each in more detail.

Brand (B)

Overview

Brand. What a loaded term these days! Branding as a marketing concept has been around for a long time and everyone tends to have different interpretations of what it means and how you can create your own. Is it a logo and your tag line? Is it your official color scheme? Is it what your members, donors, or customers think of you? When engaging in a branding discussion, the most effective marketers define what outcomes they are trying to create through branding and then guide their specific actions in support of those goals. The same thing goes for online branding strategy.

My favorite example of how this relates to a nonprofit organization website comes from one of my clients, the Ecological Society of America (ESA) (discussed in the last chapter). We were on the phone with several members, conducting a group interview as part of our research for determining the nature and direction of their new website. At one point a member said, "You know, when I look at the website I want to be proud to be an ecologist and proud of my affiliation with ESA."

That statement knocked me back in my chair as if someone had just kicked me in the chest. It crystallized ideas we had been considering as we started the project; suddenly the core strategy for their site was obvious to us all. ESA's members don't go into ecological science for the money. They do so because they are passionate about the field and want to dedicate their careers to learning and teaching about ecology. Tying that passion to the association would help with membership recruitment and retention along with many other outcomes. Using this emotional tie as a central principle for ESA's website was a perfect fit between the outcomes that ESA wanted to create and the characteristics of their website audiences. That is a great example of using brand as a central strategy for a website.

Seth Godin summed up this approach on his blog in 2007 with the following statement: "If you want to grow a valuable brand, my advice is to keep awareness close to zero among the people you're not ready for yet, and build the most predictable, emotional experience you can among those that care about you." Creating a predictable, emotional, experience for a specific audience yields the greatest positive benefits. This is a key lesson. In ESA's case, they are working to support an emotional and consistent experience with their members and potential members, not the entire world. The former is something they can achieve and do well. The latter is impossible, yet all too many organizations try to tilt that windmill with about as much success as Don Quixote.

Relevant Outcomes

Outcomes for brand-driven web strategy can be quite varied. In general, a brand strategy for your website will attempt to reinforce the overall branding of the organization or specific products and services or some combination. Sites that support branding effectively are very clear about what outcomes they are supporting.

Common branding outcomes for web strategy include

- Strengthening affiliation with the organization;
- Strengthening affiliation with the profession, field, practice, product, or industry;
- Transmitting ideas and values across the web via social media channels that are consistent with our brand; and
- Building support for and consistent with other communication channels, such as print and video.

Branding outcomes for a specific product or service will be very similar to those above but are more focused. Some organizations have events with their own strong identity, and the brand of the organization is not front and center. The Consumer Electronics Show (CES) is an example. At the time of this writing, the event's website mentions the Consumer Electronics Association and their logo but that branding is very subtle and secondary to the overall brand of the trade show.

Audience Considerations

Most web strategies are highly influenced by the audiences you wish to attract and serve. Branding is no different. In fact, the audience is paramount when determining how to best support branding outcomes online. Some questions to consider:

- Who among our markets are we trying to influence with our brand or brands?
- Which of those groups are likely visitors to our site?
- What content, design, and functionality would best support our brand with those people?
- What would be remarkable enough to motivate our website audiences to voluntarily share our content with others, facilitating the growth and health of our brand?
- Is our organizational brand relevant to the outcomes we are trying to create with these audiences?

That last question is quite helpful when considering how to address consumers or the general public online. I've helped many organizations who are wrestling with whether to make consumer-oriented content a part of their main website or to develop a completely separate site with its own identity. A key criterion in this scenario is whether the organization's brand identity is an asset to achieving your goals for audiences from the general public. If your organization's brand is irrelevant, then having a separate site makes a lot of sense. Recall the Got Milk?* campaign I mentioned earlier in the book. The sponsoring organization's identity is not key to their outcomes, so it is actually rather hard to learn who is behind the milk! Making that decision allowed the ads to focus just on the milk and avoid cluttering things up with additional brand images and messages. However, if your organization's brand *is* a significant aid in achieving your goals with public audiences, then it may make sense to integrate that into your online presence targeted at consumers.

Branding as a Driving Force or Supplemental Strategy?

Can brand be a driving force strategy for your web efforts? Certainly. When your goals online are to further the reputation and perceived value of your organization, members, industry, or other factor, then a strong branding focus may be the answer. This will mean that furthering your brand will dictate the content, design, and functionality of your site more than any other single factor.

And there's the rub; for many organizations their brand or overall brand strategy is not fully formed. In other cases, the organization has other priorities to achieve set by their board and leadership that are more pressing than sustaining the brand. When this is the case, brand is much better off as a supplemental strategy rather than the overwhelming focus of your site. There are not too many analogs to the Got Milk?* campaign, for example, that put a single industry identity truly front and center ahead of all other priorities.

Impact on Content

Content on your site is actually fairly important to a branding strategy, which may be a bit counter-intuitive. Branding often brings to mind logos and color palettes. With the web, however, you must have content to attract the audiences you wish to impact with your brand. Then the content must reinforce and support the value and emotional reaction you are trying to achieve.

Going back to the Ecological Society of America (ESA), they wanted to really hit that emotional tie to the organization and the field of ecology with their redesign. In translating that priority to their content, ESA launched a blog that tells the story of the organization and the research and education efforts of their members. They have also created a popular podcast series where ESA staff interview authors of recent journal articles, exploring the story behind their research. These are great examples of creating content that is likely to elicit the excitement and interest they are aiming for by leveraging off of their existing activities and programs.

Some questions to ask when exploring this strategy for your organization might include the following:

- What content would generate excitement and interest among our intended audiences?
- What topics among those are aligned the closest with the value we wish to convey through our branding efforts?
- Do we have that content now? If not, how could we create it or gain access to it?
- What content could our members contribute that would support our brand?

Another way that content can support and influence branding is through the information architecture of the site. In a strong brand strategy, content should be grouped and labeled to support the value you are trying to convey. For example, if a large part of the value you wish to convey via your site is the value of membership, then highlighting content and services for members in a visible way is a critical tactic. Ultimately, the content associated with a branding strategy must draw the right people and convey the right messages in order to generate the desired reaction.

Impact on Design

A variety of studies claim that website visitors make snap judgments about the quality of a site and the organization it represents in less than a second. In that amount of time, they are not parsing your content or how well your local search engine works; they are reacting to the visual design and layout of your site. I'm no cognitive scientist, but even if it takes five seconds to make that first impression, your design is going to be a significant factor in it. Given this dynamic, design is a critical element of a brand-driven web strategy.

On the obvious side, you will want the site to match and support the brand of your organization (or milk!) so that it reinforces what you are conveying in other media and experiences. This includes using your logo appropriately and choosing a color scheme that is complementary to your core visual branding rules or guides. The ideal outcome would be if a person familiar with one of your print publications comes to your website, their mind should immediately make the connection of, "Aha! This is the same group."

On the more subtle side, consider what imagery will create the emotional reactions you hope to achieve with your audiences. ESA chose to include photos of their members working in the field (literally!) along with a rotating overall design for the site that featured a different biome each month. ESA's membership covers a diverse range of environments and specialties and this changing design creates interest across the profession while also appealing to specific segments.

Impact on Functionality

Functionality relates to a branding strategy primarily in facilitating the delivery of content or media in a way that supports the specific outcomes of your branding approach. The three primary areas as they relate to nonprofits include content access, rich media delivery, and interactive applications.

Many membership organizations provide content and interactive services to members as a benefit of belonging to the organization. In these cases, it should be easy to see and assess the value of the restricted parts of the site when visitors are asked to log in. The site must show what content the user is attempting to access, including a short description, and links to learn how to gain access, all in addition to the login form. This functionality typically has to be developed within the content management system for the site. It's an important element in supporting the value of the membership message in a brand.

Rich media delivery covers content such as audio, video, and animations. Many organizations use free services such as YouTube for housing and delivering this kind of content. If that's the case for you, then your functionality requirements will be low. In some cases you may chose to develop or license software and services to deliver this content without it being branded as part of a free service. In those instances you will need to determine how to fulfill that capacity on your site. Either way, you will need to invest in software and hardware with which to create the rich content, unless you outsource this completely.

Interactive applications can vary a lot, from games to calculators to fundraising tools. Many of these applications will be designed to be easily shared or distributed to maximize their use and reach. iPhone and

Facebook applications are examples of these. Most organizations will outsource development of these stand-alone applications. In a brand strategy context, the applications must deliver and communicate the value you wish to create while making sure the users know who provided the app and how to learn more.

Impact on People

Branding strategies will have less of an impact on core web staff as they tend to be driven by higher level strategic personnel and rely on external vendors for specialized skills and needs. That said, here are several areas to consider for development in your staff when you know you will have a strong branding strategy for your web efforts.

Strategy and Marketing

Branding decisions are typically closely tied to the overall strategy of the organization and will be very influential on how marketing activities are conducted. Given that, the role of web staff will often be to interpret and implement a broader branding strategy online. Lead web staff should be involved in branding strategy discussions and, ideally, in its formulation so that they can provide input into how the online world can be leveraged to achieve the organization's objectives.

Marketing skills are also important when implementing brand strategies online. Web staff must be able communicators who can orchestrate a web presence that fully communicates the messages of the organization's brand.

If the web will be an important avenue for supporting and spreading the organization's brand then web staff must have a seat at the strategy table. To be able contributors and peers, the lead web position must be sufficiently senior to contribute meaningfully and be heard by other senior staff.

Design and Interactive Online Media

Visual design is a critical component to communicating branding messages. Your web designers must be able to partner with those who develop your overall branding direction (if they are a separate team or outside resource) in order to execute consistently with your desired outcomes. Since the visual implementation of a brand typically doesn't change too quickly or radically, you may be able to outsource this part of your design work. The greatest impact is likely to be on the overall template and design standards for the entire site. This could be implemented by an outside firm and then maintained with in-house talent on an ongoing basis. In any case, branding changes are likely to trigger an intense round of design work for a short period of time.

Likewise, designing interactive online media such as games or applications can effectively be outsourced, with in-house staff or your regular web company conducting the maintenance. If your plans call for many such applications, however, you may want to develop in-house talent for creating these since it would be more of a core capability of the team.

Video/Audio Production

Video and audio are becoming much more common in online content for all types of organizations. This richer medium can be quite powerful in creating emotional responses desired from branding efforts. If this will be a key part of your online efforts, then you will want to invest in the ability to produce and deliver this kind of content.

There are numerous inexpensive devices that produce relatively high quality video and audio files. These tools are relatively easy to learn and use by any staff person. The more complicated techniques come to play in editing the content for presentation online. If you plan to do a lot of this content, then it can make sense to get one or more staff up to speed on working with this content and how to optimize it for deployment online. If your volume of work will be relatively low or you wish to have more polished product at the end with higher production values, then it would be wise to retain an outside firm to develop video and audio content for your site.

Video and audio are also very common in social media efforts and can be an effective supplement to traditional blog content. If intended for social media use, the more important aspect of audio and video is that they are authentic and timely. Given that, you can go with much lower production values than you might for other efforts. For example, ESA uses college interns to produce all the audio for their podcast, working with open source and inexpensive software for recording and editing the interviews.

Case Study:
Patagonia, Inc.: Living Their Philosophy Online

Yvon Chouinard's book, *Let My People Go Surfing*, explores the history of Patagonia and how his business philosophy for the company grew over time. I, of course, checked out their website and was impressed with how well it embodies his and Patagonia's philosophy of business.

Patagonia's mission statement is "Build the best product, cause no unnecessary harm, use business to inspire and implement solutions to the environmental crisis." If you have seen a print catalog from the company then you have seen this in action. Each includes lots of content about protecting the environment and the actions that Patagonia and their customers have taken to do so, while enjoying all that nature provides.

As I reviewed Patagonia's website at the time of this writing, the philosophy came through loud and clear. For example:

- The home page is dominated by a dramatic picture of a climber in the mountains, an image that resonates with both Patagonia's roots and their current customer base.

- Some links go to products but many lead to information about causes the company supports and their own initiatives.

- There is exactly one product featured on the home page as of this writing.

- A blog publishes personal stories from their staff, ambassador athletes, and customers, all of which resonate with the overall mission.

Despite a soft touch on products, website sales surpassed mail order by 2004, according to Chouinard. He attributes much of their success to how true they stay to their mission. How well does your online presence embody the mission and core values of your organization, staff, and customers?

Next Action (NA)

Overview

The Next Action (NA) strategy is all about getting website visitors to *do* something very specific via the web. Every site has a plethora of potential next actions for each visitor. The power of NA as a strategy is that it identifies which of those next actions are of strategic value to the organization and should receive specific support and investment to maximize conversion. This strategy helps to focus scarce resources on outcomes of the most importance. While many other next actions will still be supported by the site, these are the ones you will measure the closest because they provide strategic value to the organization.

In this strategy, I am focusing on next actions that do not include e-commerce transactions. The Direct Sales strategy discussed earlier in the book is a specific instance of NA; however, it is such a huge area in and of itself that I decided to treat it separately. The next actions in this section might ultimately lead to an e-commerce sale or something completely different but they are distinct from DS transactions by the lack of an e-commerce component.

Relevant Outcomes

Next Action outcomes for nonprofit organizations can cover a wide range of potential activities for website visitors. Grassroots advocacy efforts are often a strategic initiative for many organizations and a prime candidate for an applied web strategy. Sites with a focus on creating and fostering online communities might have critical next actions around signing up new users and then making their first contribution to the discussions or work of the group. Others may ask visitors to recruit their friends and colleagues or share information with them. The key in all cases is to understand what next actions on the site can best support those strategic goals. Some examples of outcomes that can be supported by a next action strategy include the following:

- Submit an email address and zip code from a website visitor who wishes to support the advocacy efforts of the organization;
- Share important content from the website via social media and networking sites;
- Sign up for a free email newsletter so that subscribers can later be converted into new members;

- Submit a customized form letter to the user's congressional delegation; and
- Provide personal demographic data via the site that can be used for analysis of the entire membership for marketing purposes.

Here is a process to use for analysis of your top initiatives in order to determine which would be best served by a focused next action strategy:

- Map out the entire process for each initiative, identifying which steps require someone to willingly take some form of action;
- Of those actions, identify which could be fulfilled online; and
- Of those, note which are critical to the overall process.

That analysis will leave you with a short list of potential next actions worthy of significant online investment.

Audience Considerations

An NA strategy must focus on the specific audiences needed to actually take that next step. Online success will be hard to attain if your organization wants to influence a Senator from Indiana but you only have 10 visitors from the state! The key questions to consider for your NA audience include the following:

- Who do we need to take this next action?
- Do they already come to our site? If not, how can we get them to do so?
- If multiple audiences are candidates for this next action, do they differ in how they will want to participate or be persuaded to do so?
- Do they already take this kind of next action online or will it be a new behavior for them?

Fully understanding your audiences in the context of next actions will allow you to be much more effective in creating the results you wish to achieve. E-commerce testing techniques are equally effective in measuring success for next actions as well. Conduct split tests among different demographics to see what works and what doesn't for each. Data and measurement are your friends in determining how to best achieve your desired next step with key audiences.

Next Action as a Driving Force or Supplemental Strategy?

Next Action is often used as a supplemental strategy for another driving force. The exceptions are when the organization as a whole has one or two very specific actions they want the majority of their website visitors to take on their site. In those cases, an NA strategy could serve best as the main focus on a website. Most organizations that I've worked with will use one of the other strategies as a driving force that aligns with the core value they are trying to create and use an NA strategy to supplement. However, even in those cases, NA could be used as a temporary driving force, especially when the organization is responding to emergent issues or crises.

For example, as I am writing this paragraph, the H1N1 Flu (née Swine Flu) is a top item in the news and many nonprofits are hustling to respond. Several organizations have put together lists of resources and tips for their members and the people their members serve, and published them online. The next action they wish people in those audiences to take from their home page is to go and access those materials. Therefore, they have placed large features on the home page to draw attention and guide people to them. This is a great example of a temporary Next Action driving force strategy redefining their home page during the crisis.

"Is this next action the most important thing our site can achieve with most of our visitors?" If you answer yes to that question, then NA may make sense as a driving force strategy for your site. Otherwise, it will be a complementary strategy to some other driving force.

Impact on Content

NA strategies are all about convincing people to take that next step and then making it abundantly easy to do so. Content for next actions, therefore, will usually fall into the persuasion part of the equation, with perhaps a bit of explanatory text on what to do next. Ideally, the actual action of taking that next step is easy enough that you don't have to develop content specifically for how to do it.

Persuasive content should explain why it is in the user's best interest to take that next step. If you are asking for data, why should they give it to you? How will they be better off? In the sample objective above of securing email and zip code data for grassroot activities, it's critical to explain why giving access to their inbox for this effort will make sense.

In Robert Cialdini's classic book, *Influence: The Psychology of Persuasion*, he explores six different factors that aid in ethically persuading people to act in a desired way. Let's explore a few of those and how they might apply to your website.

Reciprocity

Reciprocity refers to your desired customer being indebted to you after being given something of value from you for free. Examples of how you might do this online could include

- Free reports or information;
- Free one-month trial online membership; and
- Other free content.

The trick to this approach is that you have to follow up with a request after the gift has been made. If you give a free report or one-month membership, you need to follow up soon with an offer to purchase another product or membership to benefit from the effect.

Social Proof

Cialdini says that one way people determine what is right is to look at what other people think is right. This social proof leads to the power of testimonials from trusted people. For your website, you might consider

- A video testimonial from a member that is displayed on your join page;
- Photos and written testimonials from others who have benefited from the organization; and
- Blog posts from members discussing the value of your organization and their participation with it.

Membership organizations have always used social proof for effective marketing. Make sure your website uses the same valuable technique.

Authority

People tend to believe authority figures, says Cialdini. Consider who are the authority figures in your field and industry and how you can promote your association with them. Often, the leadership of organizations may be these very same figures. Highlighting them in strategic positions in your site or in appeals for registration, renewal, or joining could add extra oomph to your conversion rate.

Scarcity

Opportunities appear more valuable when availability seems limited. One simple example of this on the web is Amazon.com. Often they will show a "only 5 left in stock" message for items. I am sure this is true but it may also be the case they only carry five in inventory at any one time.

Either way, they create the appearance of scarcity, further incenting someone to buy, according to Cialdini's work.

For your own site you can use the technique when you have only limited spots in a program available, only so many products left, etc. You can do this manually by editing your site and email blasts or do it systematically as Amazon does with their inventory.

Impact on Design and Functionality

I have combined design and functionality in this chapter because they really go hand-in-hand. As in direct sales, usability is a critical consideration in the design of your site as it relates to facilitating the next actions you wish your visitors to take. This will impact both the visual design and layout of your site as well as the functionality in place to complete the desired actions.

When NA is a driving force or strong supplemental strategy, the most successful organizations dedicate additional resources to the design of the relevant interfaces and forms. The design of the site should speed people through the steps you wish them to take and otherwise stay out of the way.

The most significant difference between design for an NA strategy compared to DS is that direct sales is typically a bit more complex of a transaction, since you have to gather credit card and other information to fulfill the order. NA designs will often be much simpler and therefore easier to create a usable interface.

Impact on People

NA strategies have more of an impact on your own staff than Branding may have. The actions you want to have happen will require more daily monitoring and adjustments to get the best performance and this is often best fulfilled by your own staff.

Web Analytics

Data collection and measurement are critical when attempting to create specific outcomes online. If you have a strong NA strategy in place then you will want to have staff that can not only design the right interfaces online but also measure performance as people use them. They will need to be able to configure your analytics package to track visitors as they go through your processes and look at overall success rates. They will also need to be able to communicate the results of their analysis to other staff and your vendors and work with them to make adjustments to improve on your metrics.

User Interface Design and Usability

Your staff or vendor resources for creating portions of your site focused on next actions must be expert in usability and simplicity while also achieving your business goals. Simple!

Since many next actions involve collecting data of some sort, look for staff or vendors with backgrounds in building forms that are tied to databases on the back-end. Review their prior work and try it out yourself. They should also be very open to working across teams since their applications are serving someone else's business goals in most cases.

Ultimately, the outcomes you wish to achieve and the audiences you will achieve them with must drive every design. Your designers and programmers must be able to hold both considerations in mind at the same time while creating interfaces. Those who "build to spec" are likely to deliver the worst interfaces. A good interface designer is worth a lot to your organization when NA is a key strategy.

Marketing and Sales

Background in marketing and sales can definitely benefit your web staff when formulating and implementing next action strategies. Concepts from direct marketing and sales, such as split testing, are invaluable to crafting and fine-tuning the applications, designs, and marketing campaigns that should all form a part of your integrated marketing campaigns.

Database Integration

Finally, database integration is a key attribute with next action strategies, in a very similar way to direct sales. Quite often, a successful next action will result in data that you need to store and later analyze or put to work. Staff and/or your supporting vendors must be adept at working with your core database of members or donors as well as with your online systems.

Case Study:
Jeffrey Gitomer's Shameless Next Action

Jeffrey Gitomer is one of the top marketing and sales gurus in the country. Not too surprisingly, his website focuses on moving his visitors through a variety of next actions, building their relationship with him and his body of work.

Below is a screen shot of four potential next actions that appear at the bottom of many of Jeffrey's web pages. Placing a prominent call to action at the end of a page is a great way to retain traffic from visitors who have finished reading the current page and are about to go on to other things.

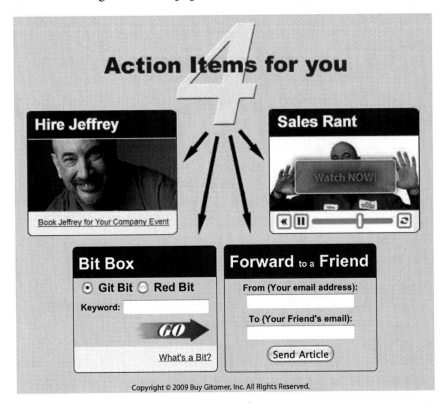

What I love about Jeffrey's approach is that he is completely and totally shameless with his next actions. Hire me! Listen to me! Share me! Use the bit box to find resources mentioned in my books!

How can you be more shameless on your website about what you want your visitors to do? It's really hard to be too over-the-top. Subtly doesn't win awards in this game.

KEY POINTS

- Brand strategies online should communicate value and create the same reactions you try to achieve with the overall brand of your organization.

- Brand strategy can also be applied to a specific product, service, or event with its own unique identity.

- Next Action as a strategy is all about moving people through to the outcomes you wish to create with your marketing.

- Next Action strategies online should be one element of an overall integrated marketing campaign for best results.

Formulating a Winning Web Strategy

NOW FOR THE FUN PART! In this chapter we will explore how to determine which of the seven potential strategies should serve as the driving force for your website and which should be used as supplemental strategies. The next chapter then goes into how you plan the implementation of the site based on the strategy you develop.

Web strategy has to be anchored to the overall strategy of the organization. In essence, your website should be one expression of your organization's overall strategic vision and direction, executing on the specific outcomes you need to realize your goals. The most effective websites, in my experience, are those that take a focused approach to achieving those strategic objectives. One way to create this focus is with a driving force web strategy. But first, let's explore overall organizational strategy and how it relates to your website and other online efforts.

Assessing Overall Organization Strategy and Operations

Your organization's overall strategy is an expression of intent. It should define how you plan to go about fulfilling your mission. With a good strategy in hand you can define what products and services you will offer to which markets in order to achieve your goals. Thoroughly understanding your top-level strategy enables you to execute a website and other online media that contribute to those goals.

The reality for your web efforts in the big picture is that they are almost completely at the tactical level. Your top strategy may mention the web and even identify it as a significant element in creating your desired outcomes. However, your organization doesn't exist to have a website. It does exist to fulfill your mission and serve your constituents. As important as the online world can be to achieving your mission, I've always found it helpful to keep it in perspective and remember that it is simply a means to your desired ends rather than a sacrosanct work of art, immune to mundane things such as marketing and sales.

Figure 2 shows the organizational and web strategy formulation stages first introduced in Chapter 2. As you can see, the organization's overall strategy is informed and shaped by the mission. You might say vision or purpose instead of mission; it doesn't really matter what label you use. It's simply why your organization was created and what you hope to achieve at the highest level possible. Let's explore how the mission and philosophy of your organization relate to web strategy.

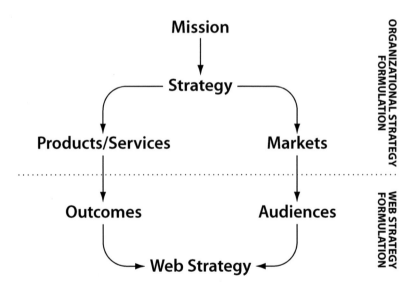

Figure 2: Organizational and Web Strategy

Mission and Philosophy

At first glance, mission is the furthest thing from implementing your website. However, there are several aspects to assess from your mission and overall philosophy or organizational culture that can be used to influence your online approach. For example, HopeWell Cancer Support, an organization that supports cancer patients and their families, has a philosophy that each participant in their program is to be treated as a person, not as a diagnosis. This informs all of their programs and actions, including their website. The design of their new site, currently under development, features images that represent their participants as regular people, completely downplaying the medical aspects of what they are dealing with.

Questions to ask of your mission, vision, culture, or philosophy as you work on your web strategy are:

- Does our mission infer any particular themes for content and design of our web presence?
- Does our mission imply certain approaches or messages to our markets?
- How should our mission inform and mold our overall brand as an organization and what impact should that have online?

Mission is something you should periodically refer back to throughout the formulation and implementation of your web strategy to make sure you are remaining consistent with the values of your organization. Ultimately, websites that support key objectives will contribute the most to realizing your vision as an organization, but it is valuable to make sure you are doing so in a way that is philosophically simpatico with the intent of your mission.

Organizational Strategy

Your overall organization strategy is a statement of your intent. It should specify what you intend to achieve to fulfill your mission. Good strategies provide an effective decision framework for determining what products and services you will offer to which markets. In the context of nonprofit organizations, your markets can include both those you serve as well as those who support or fund you in that pursuit. For membership organizations this is often the same group, while charities often raise funds from one market in order to serve another.

Products and Services

The key to interpreting organizational strategy for your website is to identify the specific outcomes the organization must achieve to support that strategy. The products and services you choose to offer will largely determine these outcomes. Many of these items will have profit associated with them while others may operate at a loss or at cost in support of your mission and underwritten by other revenue. Either way, each product or service has operational outcomes associated with it that need to be achieved. These outcomes typically fall into one of the seven strategies identified earlier in the book. Identifying these outcomes is critical to prepare for formulating your web strategy. It's like the drive train in an automobile, connecting the engine of your organization to the road, allowing you to drive with great power in pursuit of your mission and goals.

You must prioritize your products and services so you can judge which should receive the most support and investment online. There are three criteria that I've found useful in making an initial assessment: impact, total revenue, and net profit.

Total revenue and net profit are what you would expect. These figures tell us which elements of your offerings have the most significant cash flow and which are the most profitable for the organization. These measurements are usually enough with for-profit companies, but nonprofits benefit from assessing impact as well. Impact looks at how much each service or product contributes to your mission or other priorities of the organization. This allows you to assign value to items such as government relations programs, which have tremendous value for your constituents but are certainly not profit centers.

Once prioritized, you can then assess the relative importance of the outcomes each product or service needs to achieve, allowing you to determine which strategies are most closely aligned with the core value you are trying to achieve.

Markets

To continue the automotive analogy, if you see the outcomes of your products and services as the drive train, then the process of assessing your markets is like the function of the steering wheel. A clear understanding of which audiences are important for your online goals allows you to target your strategies more effectively.

The definition of your markets should be driven by your overall strategy as an organization; whom do we need to serve or engage with to achieve our mission in the way we planned?

Markets can be defined many ways and clearly understanding how you define yours will enable you to have a more effective website. Some common dimensions for market definitions in the nonprofit sector include

- Geography;
- Industry or market sector;
- Profession;
- Type of job or job level;
- Institutional affiliation;
- Socio-economic status;
- Race, religion or heritage;
- Career stage; and
- Many others too numerous to mention!

small-ticket middle markets, etc.

Understanding how you define and segment your markets gives you the knowledge you need to fine-tune your approach online. For example, I worked with one membership organization whose members are high-level executives. While the executives were a key audience for the website, it turned out their assistants handled most of their transactions with the association, such as renewing membership or registering for an event. This led to the assistants becoming another important audience for the site. This shows how you have to analyze your markets in the context of the outcomes you wish to achieve online in order to have the most success.

In analyzing your own market segments, look at how you currently market. How do you differentiate among your total potential audience? What demographics or other data do you use to differentiate among them? What seems to have the biggest impact on the results of your marketing and communication? Answering these questions will help you to refine the markets that you address, preparing you to tease out the most relevant online audiences for your efforts.

What If We Have No Discernable Overall Strategy?

Don't laugh at this heading. I have actually been asked this question more than once, how can we have an effective website if our organization has no discernable strategy? The short answer is, make up a top-level strategy and use that as your guide! Let me explain what I mean by that before you toss the book across the room.

By nature of its existence, every organization has an implied strategy. You are pursuing goals, creating products, delivering services, and targeting markets. Even when it appears you are running on autopilot, there is enough evidence for you to make an assessment of how the web and online world can be used to best support your operations. The risks of not having an intentional strategy at the top level are quite severe, because changes in our environment are rapid these days. However, you may own your website and not the top strategy of the organization and you have to start somewhere.

My philosophy is that it is always better to take some action to improve your online results, even when the organization's top direction is not entirely clear. Don't bet the farm but do create a website that is highly focused on achieving outcomes important for your current operations.

Outcomes and Audiences

During a summer in college when I was working a construction job, I once saw a prefabricated home that had been placed upon a poorly built set of basement walls. Two sides of the basement caved in after the house was set, making it possible to see daylight under the base of the building! Erecting a website without a strong foundation can lead to the same result, an online home that is on shaky ground and in which no sane person would want to live. Clearly defined outcomes and audiences for your site provide a strong foundation for online success.

The final stage before crafting your web strategy is to define the specific outcomes you must create and the audiences you must serve to achieve them. Outcomes and audiences serve as the foundation for web strategy. The better you develop this base the easier it will be to successfully implement your web strategy. Weak or nonexistent definitions for these two items will leave you with something like that poor house

I described above. The first step is to identify and prioritize your key outcomes and audiences. Before getting to that, however, I want to take a moment to define what outcomes and audience mean.

For the purposes of web strategy, an outcome is some measurable change, action, or behavior that you wish a visitor to take or experience. The significant word in that definition is "measurable." If you can't measure that an outcome has occurred, then you have little chance of knowing that you succeeded or being able to adjust your approach to improve results. The types of measure you use can vary from the heavily quantitative to more subjective. Purchases and clicks fall into the highly quantitative measures. Survey or focus groups results are more subjective. Either way, you need to have some way of measuring progress. An outcome that can't be measured is an aspiration, not a goal. Keep refining until you have a measure for each outcome. Based on the strategy model we are constructing here, the outcomes you develop that support your highest value products or services should receive the greatest prominence. I'll discuss that in a bit more detail shortly.

An audience is any group of people with some measurable characteristic in common which influences how relevant and significant they are to your specific outcomes. Measurable is a critical word again. If you can't identify them, then you can't address them online. Also critical is the relationship to outcomes. The audiences that are relevant to many outcomes and/or the highest value outcomes will then become primary audiences for your website strategy.

Identification and Prioritization

Before drafting your web strategy you must inventory your potential website outcomes and audiences and rank order them in importance. There is no magic road for doing so; whatever methodology works best for your team and leadership is fine. The outcome that your methods must achieve is a prioritized list of audiences and outcomes based on your market and the products and services you offer to them.

I have worked with clients who already had a fairly detailed high-level strategic plan that we were able to analyze to derive outcomes and audiences online. I have also worked with other clients who did not have a very detailed strategy at the highest level. In those cases, I like to focus on their operations to determine what they are currently offering and plans for the future. This can take a bit of extra effort, but you have to do it to lay a strong foundation.

Here are questions to use to surface the key outcomes for your online presence, based on your products and services:

- What is our process for creating, marketing, and delivering each product or service?
- For each stage in those processes, which could benefit the most from integration with our online presence?
- After identifying all of these outcomes, can any be combined because they are essentially the same thing?
- Whom do we need to attract and serve online for each identified outcome?

At the end of this process, you should have a list all potential outcomes your site could achieve in support of your goals and have merged like ones together. For example, if you have similar outcomes for selling three different books online, these could be combined as one outcome that applies to a class of products.

Once the list is created, you must prioritize it. Factors to consider include revenue, contribution to significant goals of the organization, and scope of impact on your total user population. The precise evaluation criteria can vary significantly between organizations. The team you have working on strategy must define a set of criteria that make the most sense given your operations and governance culture. These criteria must be justifiable to others in the organization when you defend your choices for where you will focus precious resources.

As you prioritize, look for natural breaks among the outcomes so that you can place them into no more than three tiers of importance. The first tier should include critical outcomes that have the greatest impact for supporting the products and services you offer. The second tier should include outcomes that are significant and should be addressed by your strategy but are not the primary drivers of value you need from your site. Finally the third tier should include outcomes you need to achieve but are of lesser importance than the first two. Some of them may also fall into the "nice to have" category rather than "must have." This tiered classification is hugely valuable as you assess which of the seven potential strategies will serve you best online.

Audience identification and evaluation should follow a process very similar to that of outcomes. Consider these questions to populate your initial list of potential audiences for your website:

- What audiences for our site do our target markets imply? Consider all the various ways in which you already define market segments for your organization.

- What audiences are required to achieve the major outcomes we have identified for the site?

- What audiences should we address based on our stated mission, vision, and values as an organization?

- What other audiences are relevant to our website and are not captured by any of the above? Polling key staff throughout the organization can help surface additional audiences that you might otherwise miss.

Answering these questions will get all of your potential audiences onto the table. Come up with a very short summary to describe each audience for your site, describing what makes them a uniquely identifiable audience and how many of them you estimate exist. Include any information you have about how they access the web, such as being reliant on mobile devices or only likely to go online at home on their own time rather than during working hours.

After you have your total list of audiences with their short descriptions, work on combining those that are very similar and then rank ordering them by priority. Here priority can be influenced by a number of factors that, again, will vary quite a bit from organization to organization. One criterion that everyone should use, however, is relationship to your top outcomes. Audiences that are the target of, or required for, your top-tier outcomes should be rated much higher than others.

At the end of this process, you should have two prioritized lists, the outcomes and audiences most relevant to the primary operational and strategic goals for the organization. Congratulations! Now it's time to give those lists a reality check.

The Reality Check

It can be somewhat easy for a team formulating web strategy to get out ahead of the organization or to make assumptions based on an idealized version of reality. An excellent time to insert a reality check is right after preparing your prioritized outcomes and audiences lists. Here are two tests to apply to your lists to validate them with your actual operations and make sure you have considered critical connections between the two.

Connecting Outcomes to Audiences. Place your prioritized lists of audiences and outcomes side by side and make connections between each outcome and its related audiences. Outcomes are typically the driver here. If an important outcome has no identifiable audience on your list, you need to come up with one. Likewise, if a highly ranked outcome links primarily to a low ranked audience, you may need to change one or both of those items' positions in your lists. If you have an orphaned audience or two with no corresponding outcomes, you should assess if you need to add some outcomes for them given the importance of the audience or if the audiences should be dropped from the list. Either result is valid but should be an intentional decision based on what will best support the goals of the organization at the top strategy level.

The goal of this exercise is to determine if each outcome and audience has an appropriate match on your lists and that the ratings between the two are congruent.

Compare to Actual Operations. After comparing and adjusting your lists, it's time to run them past your colleagues. You can do this formally in a structured process or informally, depending upon your style and the culture of your group. My bias is to go informal if possible because it's usually quicker and just as effective. Either way, take your lists to each major functional or programmatic area of your organization and discuss the outcomes and audiences you have come up with. Do they see anything missing from either list? Do they have significant problems with how you have rated any particular item? People are always influenced by what they work closest with so you must adjust for that. However, I've found that simply checking this set of lists against staff who had not worked on its development is very valuable in both confirming your work and pointing out areas that you have missed.

That done, you are now ready to formulate your web strategy! I'll touch briefly on the concept of driving force strategy for the web and then go into how to use a web strategy profile to explore which mix of the seven web strategies will best serve your goals.

Driving Force Web Strategy

Chapter 2 gave an overview of the driving force concept but I would like to revisit it in a bit more detail before moving on. Zimmerman and Tregoe introduced us to the concept of driving force strategy in their book, *Top Management Strategy*. I have adapted their idea—that every organization has a driving force that influences the nature and direction of the business more than any other—and applied it to the world of creating effective websites and online media. A driving force web strategy is the one strategy out of the potential seven that best meets the primary goals of your organization. It is a statement of intent about how you chose to create value online and what that will mean for the content, design, and functionality of your site.

Choosing a driving force from the different strategy categories (revenue, market needs, and marketing) can make a huge difference in your strategy and overall website results. This is the beauty of selecting a driving force from among the seven strategies; you can make a real choice about what focus online will create the best results for your organization. The one thing that poorly performing websites almost always have in common is a lack of focus. These sites attempt to achieve too many objectives at the same time, leading to mediocre results across the board, at best.

In practice, the driving force web strategy will determine the content, design, and functionality of your site more than any other single factor. This is the key to creating a site that will deliver breakthrough results for your organization.

After determining your driving force strategy you will need to select the other strategies you use to a lesser degree to guide the implementation of your site. These complementary strategies can enhance your core strategy as well as achieve specific outcomes that are important to your organization, if not the top priority. A key tool in developing and presenting this mix of strategies is the web strategy profile.

The Web Strategy Profile

A web strategy profile is a simple chart that illustrates the degree to which you will use each of the seven web strategies identified in this book. The seven strategies are listed across the bottom, in order by category. The vertical axis shows to what extent you will emphasize each strategy. The four levels are Nil, Weak, Strong, and Driving Force. A strategy at the driving force level, and only one can be so, will dictate the content, design, and functionality of your site more than any other single factor. A Strong strategy will also figure significantly but will complement rather than over-rule the driving force strategy. Weak strategies are there to accommodate outcomes that need to be achieved but are not of critical importance to the organization. Finally, Nil strategies are those that are of low enough value that they should not be considered much at all in the development of the site. My concept for the Web Strategy Profile was inspired by the work of W. Kim Chan and Renée Mauborgne in *Blue Ocean Strategy* in which they use a strategy canvas to illustrate strategic intent. I provide more structure and defined options in the Web Strategy Profile, which I find useful in framing the discussion around the strategic intent of nonprofit websites.

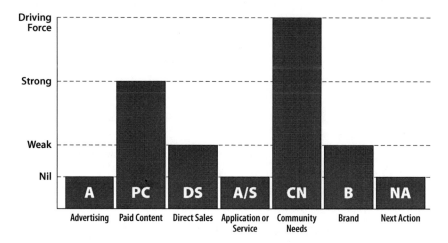

Figure 3: Sample Web Strategy Profile

The sample profile shown in Figure 3 could represent a membership organization that wants to use the needs of their community as the primary driver of the content they publish to their site. The strong secondary strategy of paid content implies that they anticipate making a fair amount of the content and services for their community available only to members. Finally, weak strategies of direct sales and branding indicate that the organization will also sell products other than content access online, although that isn't their primary goal, and they wish to make sure the site is consistent with the overall brand of the organization. That shows the power of a strategy profile; it quickly tells the story of what an organization intends to do online to create value for the organization and its constituents.

Your final strategy profile that you agree to implement functions as a communication and planning tool. It can be shared throughout your organization to educate staff and leadership on what you intend to do online, and it can be invaluable to bring partners and vendors up to speed on your intent. Your web team will use it to plan their implementation of the site (more on that in the next chapter).

Case: Virginia Association of REALTORS Web Strategy Profile

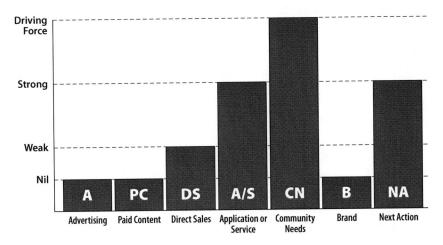

Figure 4: Virginia Association of REALTORS Web Strategy Profile

Figure 4 shows the web strategy profile that the Virginia Association of REALTORS (VAR), developed under the leadership of Ben Martin, CAE, as part of their process to determine how to best serve their members online. VAR is part of a federated membership model and does not actually sell membership directly. Their primary focus is on creating a better business environment for Realtors in their state and providing programs and services in pursuit of that mission. This led to their choice of Community Needs as a driving force strategy for their online efforts. VAR has led the way in use of social media to push content and services to their members and engage their participation. However, these early efforts were not well integrated into their central web presence. The CN strategy will enable them to continue to harness that strength in pursuit of supporting the community of REALTORS in Virginia, while making it a core part of their members' experience with them online.

The strong supplemental strategies, Next Action and Application or Service, reflect two key programs: government relations, and marketing tools. The association lobbies on behalf of the members at the state level and often asks members to take specific actions to support these goals. This is the focus of the NA strategy. VAR also provides several online services that help their members market to current and potential customers. A/S as a strong strategy reflects their desire to continue to support these outcomes for their members.

Finally, the weak Direct Sales strategy primarily supports registration for VAR's meetings and events and some product sales. Given the narrow scope and relative importance, they decided to make that a minor strategy that needed to be met but without a massive investment in the total scope of the website.

Crafting Your Web Strategy Profile

A significant question at this stage is, how do we create our own web strategy profile? Another would be, how do we know we have the one that is the best fit for us? Glad you asked! Let's delve into those key questions.

How Do You Know You're Done?

First, how do you know you have the right profile for your organization? The glib answer is, when you decide that you have. Web strategy is a statement of intent. The framework and process given in this book enable you to quickly identify the questions you must answer and the decisions you must make in order to focus your site on creating the most value possible for your organization. When you get to the stage of crafting a profile, it should rapidly become apparent which strategies are candidates for driving force, strong, weak, and nil levels. It then becomes a question of intent as to the level at which you place each strategy. At some point you make the call. This may be by consensus decision of your strategy team or it may be a single executive making the call. If this sounds somewhat messy and open to interpretation, then you have the right impression! Strategy should be born of debate and decisions. This process can be messy but that's how it goes. If your team forms your strategy without any significant differences of opinion along the way then you are probably not trying hard enough!

How to Craft Your Profile

Crafting your strategy profile should be an iterative and comparative process. The best results come when the key decision makers and implementers for your web strategy go through multiple potential profiles, assessing how well each supports the online outcomes you identified earlier in the strategy process. This debate and exploration accomplishes two critical tasks: one, insuring you consider a wide variety of options and, two, establishing buy-in and support from key stakeholders for the profile you ultimately choose to implement.

Rate the Seven Strategies by Outcomes Served

Rate each of the seven strategies by how well they serve your desired outcomes in each priority tier. This will show which are your best potential candidates for a driving force strategy and which are likely supplemental strategies. One simple but effective method for rating is to create a scoring matrix with the seven strategies on one axis and your outcomes on the other (see sample below). The outcomes should be listed in descending order of priority. Place an "X" at each intersection where a strategy would provide significant value to an outcome. The material in the earlier chapters will help you to understand which strategies will best support your outcomes. This is an important step; a lot of my consulting work involves helping my clients to determine those intersections. Based on this exercise, you should have one or two clear candidates for your driving force strategy and several others for supplemental strategies. Be sure to keep in mind your original ratings.

	OUTCOME 1	OUTCOME 2	OUTCOME 3	OUTCOME 4
Direct Sales				
Paid Content				
Advertising				
Application or Service				
Community Needs				
Brand				
Next Action				

Sample Outcome Rating Matrix

Selecting a Driving Force Strategy

How to best choose your driving force? Here are the main questions to ask about your top outcomes and audiences:

- Which of the seven strategies would do the most to drive our top outcomes?
- Which of the seven strategies is most congruent with the value we need to offer to our top audiences?
- If the website could only implement one of the seven strategies, which would we choose?

You get the idea. Search for the strategy that delivers the most value for your top goals (or the most outcomes of your entire list, inclusive of the top goals), and make that your driving force.

If you have multiple candidates for your driving force strategy, create a strategy profile for each as the driving force. How would this impact your choice of supplemental strategies? What would each imply for your online operations? Which seems to be best aligned with your mission and operational goals? Visualizing the two competing profiles in this way can help your team make an informed decision for the main driver of your online strategy.

Ultimately, if you have two essentially equal competitors for driving force, you have an opportunity to make a decision of intent. How do you intend to achieve your top goals? Selecting one driving force allows you to create a focused effort to achieve it with specific methods. This focus is enormously valuable for online success. In many cases, either strategy could lead to success. You simply have to decide which one you are going to use. It's not magic, it's creating strategic intent and then executing upon it.

Identifying Supplemental Strategies

An equally important task at this stage is to select the additional strategies that you will use to supplement the driving force strategy for your online efforts. There are two primary reasons to select a supplemental strategy for inclusion in your profile and execution:

1. The additional strategy is needed to achieve outcomes and goals that your driving force strategy doesn't directly address.
2. The additional strategy complements the driving force strategy by feeding into it or otherwise enhancing the total value it will create or improving the odds of success.

While either reason is often enough to include a supplemental strategy you should look for those that actually achieve both, because this will return the greatest results. In fact, this is a key criterion for a strong supplemental strategy; it is one that both supports the driving force of your website as well as accomplishes key outcomes that would not be otherwise supported. Let's explore some more criteria for strong, weak, and nil levels of supplemental strategies.

Strong Supplemental Strategy Criteria

- The strategy complements or enhances the potential value of your driving force strategy. Providing content that serves the specific needs of your community or market in order to have more people to sell products to is an example of using a Community Needs strategy to feed into a driving force of Direct Sales. A strong supplemental may also achieve outcomes other than those addressed by the driving force, making an even stronger case for inclusion.

- You have top- or middle-tier outcomes for the site that are not directly served by your chosen driving force strategy. For example, if your driving force strategy is facilitating Next Actions in support of your advocacy campaigns, yet you must underwrite the expense of the site via sponsorships, you could chose Advertising as a strong supplemental strategy. This serves as a strong supplemental strategy because it supports a significant outcome for the site but it has very little to do with achieving the direct outcomes related to your driving force.

Weak Supplemental Strategy Criteria

- You have middle- or bottom-tier outcomes that are not served by the driving force or strong supplemental strategies, yet still need to be addressed. A common example with scientific organizations is the need to support journal editors, authors, and reviewers. They are not key to the primary online outcomes around publishing and selling journal content, yet they need to have their processes supported online for the effective operation of the organization.

- You choose not to emphasize a certain outcome but want to apply some resources to it. This is a very valid decision to make. A good strategy helps you to make choices about where to invest scarce resources. You might move a weak strategy selected in this scenario to a stronger position later when other goals have been achieved or the focus of the organization changes in the future.

Nil Supplemental Strategy Criteria

- The main criterion is that a strategy serves no outcomes on your list directly.
- You may also decide that a bottom-tier outcome is not worth supporting directly. Again, that is a very valid decision and a key part of setting strategy for organizational websites. Deciding not to do something is often as valuable as deciding to do something; it frees up resources and allows you to create focus in other more important areas. A Nil strategy is often evidence of successful prioritization and discipline, not of an incomplete strategy.

. . . .

Profile Generation Exercise: Red/Blue Team

Here is an effective and fun exercise for designing competing strategy profiles for your online efforts. Split the group working on your strategy into two teams, Red and Blue. The Blue Team represents your organization as it is now. They are tasked to create a web strategy profile that will best serve the outcomes and audiences you have already identified and prioritized. The Red Team is the competition. They exist to eat your lunch and smile while they are doing so. They should consider themselves a start-up organization, one without the history, momentum, and limitations that your organization currently has. They are free to invent a strategy that they believe will best serve those same outcomes and audiences in the context of a new organization or company.

Send each group to different rooms and have them develop their strategy profile. Bring the groups together and have each team present their profile and why they think it will be successful. Once done, remix the participants into two new teams to evaluate the two options and which they would choose. They may also develop a third alternative if they think that is the best path. Report out again.

At the end of this process you should have several viable options for a web strategy profile and a good start on choosing what will best support your desired goals. This exercise is modeled on the U.S. Army's practice of running mock battles with one unit behaving as the enemy and the other as the Army.

. . . .

Who Should Be Involved?

I am often asked who should be involved in formulating web strategy. The most important thing to know about strategies is that they don't fail during your strategy meeting; they fail as you attempt to implement them. The single greatest cause of failed strategies is lack of buy-in from key people whose full support you need without having to hold a stick over their heads. You must have commitment to your strategy from these key players rather than simple compliance. Compliance only lasts as long as you are watching them while commitment will be sustained on its own.

The need for commitment will help you to determine who should be in the room as you develop strategy. This almost always includes a number of senior executives as well as the top managers who will have to actually implement the strategy. As you plan the group, identify who generates the most revenue online, who cares the most about the website, and who you absolutely must have onboard in order to succeed. That should get you to the group that you need.

Another important question is whether and how to involve the board of directors or other leadership group in the strategy formulation process. These leaders can definitely have a role but it is very important to be clear and precise about what you are asking them to do. If the organization has substantial staff resources and leadership, the board or other leaders can be used to inform and validate the translation of organizational strategy to web strategy, but usually will not be directly involved in the development of the web strategy. Smaller organizations with few staff may have more direct involvement of leaders from the board or a committee or task force dedicated to the project. The process in this book works with anyone. The important thing to do with volunteer leaders is to educate them on what role and contributions you are asking them to make for the project. This avoids disappointment and resentment when their expectations do not match yours.

When to Formulate Web Strategy

Organizations that have not put much effort into formulating and implementing a coherent web strategy can almost always benefit from doing it right away and then assessing what they should start and stop doing online in order to create the most value possible. However, there are several events and milestones that may trigger assessing your web strategy.

Anytime your organization has completed a top-level strategy process or assessment is an excellent opportunity to review your web strategy. Changes at the highest level almost always result in a new mix of products and services, which should then flow to the outcomes you are trying to achieve online. If you know a big strategy review is coming up, budget and allocate time for revisiting your web operations shortly thereafter.

Regardless of top-level changes, it is a good idea to annually review your web strategy and make sure it still best serves the outcomes and audiences for your site. It is not uncommon for a new product or service to be introduced during the course of a year and others to be dropped or deemphasized. These gradual changes must be accounted for in your web operations as well.

Quarterly and monthly reviews of the alignment between your online operations and strategy are useful management processes to make sure you remain focused on your top outcomes and audiences. The day-to-day work of running a website can leave you deep in the weeds. Schedule time to step back, take a deep breath, and look at the big picture.

The above events and processes can certainly be shifted or deployed in other ways than I have outlined here. The important thing is that you consciously pay attention to larger changes in the organization and take the time to think strategically throughout the year. Strategy is really best approached as a process, rather than an event.

The next chapter delves into how to implement your shiny new strategy online.

KEY POINTS

- The products and services you offer must define the outcomes you wish to pursue online.
- Audiences for your site should be a subset of your total market and greatly influenced by the outcomes you need to achieve online.
- A driving force strategy is a statement of intent: how you plan to go about creating the most significant outcomes online.
- You cannot pursue all strategies equally; deciding priorities is the whole point of the strategy formulation process.

CHAPTER 7

Implementing Web Strategy

THIS CHAPTER WILL GIVE YOU direction on planning the implementation of your web strategy. It is not a chapter on all the specific details of developing and deploying a revised or completely new website. This will get you off to a strong start and provide a road map for moving forward by identifying the key questions and topics to cover in your planning.

To review the strategy process, below is Figure 5 which shows how web strategy formulation shifts to implementation. Your web strategy, as determined by your web strategy profile, drives the content you publish,

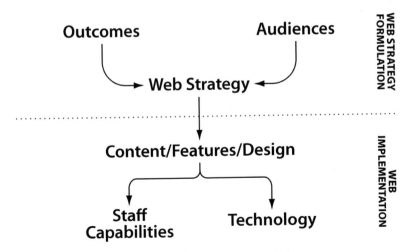

Figure 5: Web Strategy Formulation and Implementation

the design it is presented in, and the functionality that the site supports. This creates a strong and direct connection to the mission of the organization down through products and services and ultimately the site you publish.

Before delving into those elements, I do want to discuss the single most important thing you can do to provide the greatest chance of success.

The One Thing You Must Do to Successfully Implement Your Web Strategy

Here is the secret to a successful website implementation. Do this one thing and you will have done more to ensure success than almost any other action could contribute. Ready? Here it is:

- Place one person definitively in charge of the site and hold that individual accountable for success or failure.

Someone must own this baby. Someone on your staff, ideally rather high up, has to be held accountable for the success of implementing your strategy. If it fails or gets hopelessly delayed, there needs to be a single person who will have to face the music. That person should also receive fame and fortune for success (as much as you can get out of HR, in any case!).

Committees are never held accountable. Ever. If you personally know of a committee that has been held accountable for failure, in that there were personal ramifications for each and every member, please email me at david@highcontext.com. I would like to hear about it!

When I encounter committees charged with developing a website, without the benefit of an individual who owns the thing, it almost always results in a site that tries to do everything and ultimately does nothing well. You know these sites. You may even have one right now. This book is about avoiding that fate. Putting a committee in charge of developing your site will waste all of the thought and effort you put into developing your strategy. Please don't do it!

Driving Content, Functionality, and Design with Strategy

This is the real meat in translating strategy to reality. I have found that a relatively simple matrix is a great tool for determining what content, functionality, and design you need to develop and deploy in order to fulfill your strategy. The matrix consists of three columns across the top, one each for content, functionality, and design. The right-hand side of the matrix has a row for each strategy in your profile that is not at the Nil level. Put the driving force strategy at the top of the list, then your strong supplemental strategy and weak at the end. Within the matrix you can now outline the impact of each strategy on the content, functionality, and design of your site. Review each of the chapters on the different strategies for guides to the specific impact each may have on content, functionality, and design. In addition to that, here are some general questions to guide your planning as well.

	CONTENT	FUNCTIONALITY	DESIGN
Community Needs			
Application or Service			
Next Action			
Direct Sales			

Content, Functionality, and Design (CFD) Matrix example based upon the Web Strategy Profile in Figure 3.

Content

- What types of content will we publish? Examples include articles, blog posts, audio, video, short marketing copy, product descriptions, etc. Also consider if you will have significant user-generated content on your site.

- What topics do we need to cover? Should we develop a specific taxonomy with which to categorize the content and facilitate planned functionality?

- What content do we already have online? How much will we retain and how much is no longer relevant?

- Where will the content come from? Who will write it? At what frequency?

Functionality

- What functionality for website visitors is required to achieve our specific outcomes?

- What functionality do we need on the back-end to support our business processes and running of the site?

- Can we meet these needs with existing technology or off-the-shelf products or will it require custom development?

- Can we use our existing technology for our new strategy or will we need to replace or supplement it with new systems?

Design

- What imagery will best support our strategies and resonate appropriately with our target audiences?

- Does our mix of strategies require highly efficient interactive interfaces?

- Will we need to create rich and interactive media in order to achieve our goals?

Mapping out each area against your chosen strategies will quickly give you a high-level road map of what you will need to create online to make your vision a reality.

Synergy Is Your Friend

As you complete the CFD Matrix, keep an eye out for synergies. Obviously, items related to your driving force strategy will receive priority. However, be sure to look for items in each area that are very similar or essentially the same thing. These overlaps allow you to achieve more with a single effort and will make fulfilling your strategy that much easier. Content for one strategy may be equally applicable to another, or functionality to meet one need can be repurposed with minor adjustments to serve another. You get the idea.

Now You Can Talk About Technology

With the CFD Matrix completed, you can finally get to the specific underlying technology you will use for your site. Discussing functionality in the matrix gets you started but now you can begin to assess specific platforms, tools, packages, and services to use for implementing your site. The key to evaluating the technology options is to tie them to the outcomes you must create and evaluate them on the importance of the strategy they support. The more important the strategy the more you should be willing to invest in technology that supports it. For example, if direct sales of conference registrations is your driving force strategy, a major part of your investment should go into systems and technology that give you powerful tools for making those sales online. Again, this kind of prioritization is a pretty simple concept but very powerful in application.

At this stage of the game, I often find that identifying classes of technology that will fulfill the strategies and outcomes you are pursuing online, rather than zeroing in on specific products, works best. Focusing this early on a specific product or company might cause you to miss another that actually better serves your needs. Here are several classes of technology that might be relevant to your site. This is certainly not an exclusive, or even extensive list but it does cover the basics:

- *Content management system.* Pretty much a pre-requisite for any site, this helps you to edit, manage, and publish online content and present it to your website visitors. These systems may also include interactive features for website users to post comments and share your content via social media channels.

- *E-commerce.* If you sell stuff (and you probably do!) or otherwise accept money you will need a system for doing so online. These systems can be hosted or installed software and may be stand-alone or integrated with your databases and accounting systems. The extent to which you do so should be dictated by the needs of implementing your strategy.

- *Search.* Sometimes included in the content management system, this is the tool your visitors use to search your content. This is often worthy of some investment to create a good user experience and to support critical outcomes for the site.

- *Data collection and integration.* Many strategies rely on collecting some data from users via the website. This might be as simple as signing up for a newsletter or as complex as participating in a grassroot advocacy program.
- *Community and collaboration tools.* Many organization websites support interaction and collaborative work among their users. This can be a range from a simple wiki to a full-blown community platform.

Your high-level implementation plan should detail the classes of technology that you anticipate needing to implement your strategy and how they will fulfill those specific outcomes. From this you will be able later to develop specific technical requirements, requests for proposals, and other tools with which to achieve these needs.

Before I move to talking about staff, I want to address those of you who are now asking, "What? Is that all you have to say about technology?!?!" In short, yes, it is! While the web is a technology-driven medium, you don't have to get down into the weeds to map out what you need to do online to achieve your goals. The nitty-gritty details of the technology are ultimately important but not what you need to be worried about at this stage. Identifying the classes of technology and the purposes they serve in your strategy is enough for you to either put your staff to work or hire a supplier to make it happen for you. That is why we have technical professionals in the first place!

Staff

Planning how to staff your website based on your strategy is even more critical than getting the right technology. Without the people to make it happen all the fancy software in the world won't do you much good. The key is to hire and develop people with the right talents put to the right tasks, all in support of your strategic goals.

Review the staff impact described in the three strategy chapters earlier in the book. Those give you very clear ideas of the types of tasks web staff will pursue and what abilities they will need. Use the implied rankings of driving force, and strong and weak supplemental strategies to assess where you can have the most impact with staff. What skills cover the most strategies and outcomes? Which are aligned with your driving force strategy? Based on those critical factors you can determine the competencies you will need and begin to plan for lining up the best people to support them.

A great place to start is by identifying your existing staff strengths and seeing how you can leverage them. For example, if your IT team is highly versed in Microsoft technology and systems, I believe it makes all sorts of sense to favor the selection of technology on that platform if it helps you to achieve your strategic goals and can be balanced against budget and other factors used in the selection process. It will save you a lot of training and development that a system on a platform less known by your team would require.

Another factor to consider is what you can keep on staff and what you can outsource. Outsourcing is often quite cost effective, especially given the rising costs of overhead these days. One criterion to use in evaluating the top competencies for your site is the frequency at which they must be done. Actions that must happen frequently and repeatedly may be best served by a dedicated staff person. Actions that happen infrequently can often be outsourced to experts in that area who you call upon as needed. For example, redesigning the look and feel of your site is usually a rare event and could be handled by an outside firm. Authoring and posting content several times a week to a blog would probably best be served by a staff person. You get the idea.

Ultimately, your staffing and outside resources must be focused on creating the specific outcomes you need to achieve. The guidance in the strategy chapters will help you to focus those resources on the most productive abilities and accountabilities for your online presence.

The Web Team Manifesto

Insanely great web teams have the following characteristics:

- Create value, innovate, and have fun doing it.
- Help others to achieve their goals by applying web-based tools and techniques to concrete business problems.
- Do not exist to create governance processes and approval work flows, although they may use them judiciously.
- Rarely say, "No."
- Often ask, "What are you trying to achieve and what does success look like?"
- Read Godin and Drucker.
- Focus on outcomes before technology.

- Are viewed as key contributors to successful projects rather than bureaucrats to be avoided or overcome.
- Are organizational ninjas, going below the radar to solve problems much larger than their specific brief.
- LOVE the web and dig into new and experimental technology and techniques on the job and off!
- Pursue important goals rather than lowest common denominator agreement.

Does your web team meet the spirit of this list, if not the letter? Breakthrough results require a team that is focused on *creating* results rather than bureaucracy.

On The Lone Webmaster

Webmaster is a title that came about in the early days as an administrative contact for a website. It would be the person who answered webmaster@yoursite.com and made sure the server was running, updated pages, added new ones, etc. One person did it all because the domain of knowledge to create all you needed on a site was not too huge back then. The potential return on investment for a good site was also much lower back then for most organizations.

As the web matured, the roles needed for a successful site exploded, graphic design, markup, programming, content authoring and editing, information architecture, marketing, and others. Each of those roles became more complex as more tools and techniques became available and users became more sophisticated in their use of the web. The potential return for an excellent site exploded, justifying investment in more people with specialized skills and knowledge.

Except for the smallest of operations and the most exceptional of people, it is almost impossible to find someone who can do all these things competently at the same time. But organizations still try to create "do it all" jobs on the cheap. Here's a tip: People who are competent in all those disciplines are highly valuable and they are savvy to impossible jobs. You aren't going to get them.

Running a website today is a team effort, even if you have just a single person in-house managing your site. They most likely work with outside talent and resources to design your site, keep it up and running, add features, and other tasks. Given that, the title for a one-person shop position should probably be something along the lines of Manager, Director, or Producer.

In planning the implementation of your web strategy, if you have only a single staffer to dedicate to the site, determine what they must be able to do to best run the entire show and what can be outsourced to vendors, consultants, contractors, and other resources. Don't expect one person to do everything you need; they simply cannot do it any longer.

Documenting Your Plan

In my experience leading and guiding numerous technology implementation projects, I've found that less is more in documentation. A huge pile of documentation does not mean that you have done your job better or that your supplier has. It does mean you have a lot of stuff to read in order to dig out the very few bits that you need to know to make decisions. In documenting your implementation plan, there are two short documents that are about all you need to get started. These documents are the Strategy Statement and the Web Design Brief.

The Strategy Statement is typically about one page long, maybe two if you include an image of your web strategy profile. The document should state your primary outcomes and audiences for the site and your chosen strategies for achieving them. The team that works on your strategy formulation must wholeheartedly support the intent of this document. Boiling it down to this short statement makes it easy to understand and communicate within your organization and to your various vendors and partners who will work with you to implement it.

The Web Design Brief is a longer document that includes the Strategy Statement plus your assessment of the impact it will have on your content, design, and functionality, and a description of the technologies and staff abilities you anticipate needing to make it happen. In general, it should be no more than 10 pages in length. If you'd like a somewhat arbitrary rule of thumb; if it needs more than a paper clip to bind it, start cutting. The purpose of the Web Design Brief is to communicate your intent for the site in enough detail that a prospective vendor, designer, or even your own IT department could intelligently respond to how they would go about helping you to achieve your vision and the breakthrough results you desire. It should also help you to begin scoping out the implications for how you will manage the site, from processes to staff to outsourced assistance.

The precise format and outline of the brief is not too important; do what makes sense given your process. In general, use the overall strategy formulation and implementation process visual as an outline, as it is discussed here. I have provided sample high-level outlines for both documents to help you get started.

Incremental vs. Redesign

With your strategy formulated and your implementation planned at a high level, you are ready for a big question. Should you throw out your old site and start over or simply revise what you have to better serve your new goals? Here are a few salient factors in making that decision:

- **How well has the site been maintained over the past two years?** If your team has actively maintained and developed your current site then it should be in relatively good shape. Making a few adjustments to meet your new strategic direction could be enough. If the current site is a neglected basket case, there may not be enough that is salvageable and you'll have to start over.

- **Can your current technology be adapted to your new needs?**
  If the technology you already have in place can be modified to achieve your new outcomes, then a modest change to the current site may suffice for your goals.

- **Budget.** If the coffers are empty enough to not support a full redesign and new technology you have no choice. In this scenario, look for how you can modify the current site to get the most important bits of your new strategy implemented and put off lower priority goals into the future when you have the resources to pursue them.

Show Me the Money!

Budgeting for your website falls into two general types: ongoing and redesign. Ongoing budget support should cover things such as staff, outsourced resources, hosting, maintenance and support agreements for technology, and other items required to keep your site up and running and performing well. Redesign budget is money specifically allocated to update or completely replace your existing website.

Ongoing budgets vary widely and are often a function of the size of your organization and the relative importance placed upon web operations. It is easy to overlook the ongoing expenses required to keep your current site humming along while you are in the midst of figuring out how to replace it entirely. Always plan this out after devising your strategy but before investing in a redesign. The best site in the world won't do you much good if you can't afford to maintain it. You don't want to be like the game show contestant who wins a new car and then has to sell it for cash because they can't afford the taxes and insurance on the windfall.

Budgeting for a revamp or redesign of your website always raises the question of how much you can expect to spend. The investment will be determined by the technology you ultimately need and the expertise and assistance you require to create the site, including design and content development. All of these variables have a huge impact on what you will invest in and to what degree. When working with outside providers (rather than doing the work in-house with your own staff) I've seen everything from budgets of $25,000 to well into the hundreds of thousands. In general, the budget will track with the size of the organization's overall budget, since complexity and the total requirements tend to go up proportionally.

Ultimately, a redesign should be driven by a change in strategy. The same goes for budget; it should be an output of your chosen strategic direction online rather than your starting point. Once you have your strategy, look at the available budget and consider if you can achieve it given the resources you are likely to have available. Sometimes you can get pretty creative and do a lot without a huge budget but you won't know until you do the strategy legwork first.

The reality is that web strategy projects often do start with a pot of money that was allocated for the site. If that is what you have to work with, look at that number briefly and then try to forget about it while you devise your strategy. Do not limit any ideas or concepts because you think you might not be able to afford them. You won't know until later in the process, so eliminating them early may simply limit how much value you can create online with the budget you have.

When interacting with outside vendors you are considering to help you with your site, I am always in favor of disclosing to them the budget you have available. Firms that are out of your league will withdraw and those for whom your budget falls into their sweet spot will actively pursue your business. This is a good outcome! Hiding your budget simply delays things and wastes a lot of time both for you and the providers that will not be a good fit.

Finally, this strategy process will give you very good ammunition for increasing your budget to fund site development and maintenance. When done well, you will have clearly identified outcomes the site will create to serve the core of your organization's mission and purpose. Outcomes draw money. When someone tells you they don't have money available to fund the site it means that they don't see the value in doing so. There is always money available if you demonstrate enough value.

Sample Timeline for a Total Redesign Project

Sometimes you just have to toss the baby and the bathwater out together and start over. In those scenarios you are often facing a rather large and complex project! Addressing all the details and convolutions of such work is beyond the scope of this book. However, below I provide a high-level outline of the major milestones and tasks associated with a complete redesign and re-launch of your web presence. I include timing for each phase but those will vary dramatically (and I do mean dramatically!) between organizations, depending upon how many moving parts there are and the extent to which the organization can dedicate their own staff resources. This timeline also assumes using a primary vendor for most of the project. In many cases there will be two or three different vendors or suppliers involved for different elements of the site, which adds to the complexity and time as well. Finally, some elements can run concurrently, which can shorten the overall time to completion.

Thus slathered in caveats, here is the sample timeline for a total website redesign project.

Milestone 1: Vendor Assessment and Selection (4 to 8 weeks)
- Identify initial candidates based on strategy and high-level requirements.
- Conduct interviews/demonstrations of technology/design.
- Narrow field to 3 or 4 candidates and invite proposals. Give structure for responses but don't go crazy with an overly prescriptive RFP.
- Review proposals and conduct detailed demonstrations with best candidates.
- Select winning candidate.

Milestone 2: Vendor Discovery and Specifications (2 to 4 weeks)
- Winning vendor conducts detailed discovery and writes specifications for project.
- Vendor proposes fee and contract for project.

Milestone 3: Contract Negotiation (2 weeks)
- Vet proposed agreement with legal if necessary.
- Strike or revise objectionable language.
- Negotiate fee if necessary.
- Sign agreement.

Milestone 4: Design and Information Architecture (8 weeks)
- Develop detailed content inventory, flagging what to keep, revise or delete.
- Develop detailed information architecture for the new site, identifying any new content that must be created.
- Develop design concepts, revise and approve final overall template.
- Review, revise, and approve alternate templates and key landing page layouts.
- Determine and plan content workflow processes based on new information architecture.

- Identify who will write what content at what frequency when the site is live.

Milestone 5: Functionality Build-Out (8 to 12 weeks, highly variable)

- Install and configure base content management and other systems developed or implemented by vendor.
- Review, revise, and approve mock-ups of custom functional interfaces.
- Vendor develops custom applications.
- Test, debug, and approve developed custom applications.

Milestone 6: Content Migration (4 weeks, highly variable)

- Migrate content from old site into new site.
- Develop and deploy new content as needed.
- Review, revise, and approve final content for launch.

Milestone 7: Final Testing and Launch Preparation (1 to 2 weeks)

- Develop launch plan with vendor.
- Test new site on production equipment and fully installed server environment.

Milestone 8: Launch (1 day)

- Cut over domains and launch new site.
- Monitor traffic and website applications.
- Promote launch via email, press release, and social media channels as appropriate.
- Pop a cork and celebrate!
- Now, get back to work on achieving your breakthrough results.

KEY POINTS

- The content you publish, the design you present it in, and the interactive features you deploy are your answers to how you are going to achieve your web strategy.

- The single most important key to success in implementing web strategy is that one person must be in charge of the site and held accountable for performance.

- Technology is the last thing to consider and should be determined by your decisions about content, design, and functionality.

- Budget should be driven by strategy, not the reverse.

- Play to your existing staff strengths whenever you can.

- Less is more in documentation!

Getting Practical About Your Breakthrough

I AM CLOSING OUT THE BOOK with two cases and my best advice for actually achieving your breakthrough results online. Strategy is the key to success but you still need to get your organization through the door to realize results. This chapter will help you to accelerate your progress in formulating and implementing web strategy for your organization.

Stacking the Deck: Maximizing Your Chance for Success

Before embarking upon your own strategy formulation project, create your own analysis of what is working in your favor and what will hold you back. Who is in your corner and who might oppose you? Consider how you can best leverage those factors that support your success and put plans into action that will minimize or completely vitiate those that oppose you. While ushering a strategy project can be challenging at times, there is no rule that it has to be any harder than necessary! Do some up-front leg work to smooth the path to success. It is a great investment for this or any other significant endeavor. Below are some of the most common factors that I have seen in my work that can aid or hinder your project.

Factors in Your Favor
- Participation of senior executive team in web strategy formulation.
- The website is a high priority for the board of directors or other significant body of leaders.
- This book, if I may be so immodest!
- Forging agreement on priority outcomes rather than lowest common-denominator laundry lists.
- Leadership and ownership of the site.
- Sufficient staff and money for implementation.

Factors Working Against You
- Politics and turf battles.
- Extremely labor-intensive governance processes.
- Lack of senior support.
- Poor or no top-level strategy.
- No accountability.
- Lack of resources to implement your strategy.

Identify your own unique factors and make sure to pile them high on the supporting side and knock them down on the other.

Another tip for those of you who work in larger organizations is that getting IT, Finance, and HR in your corner tends to make any project much easier to achieve. Strong relationships with these three departments will help you with funding, staff, and infrastructure technology. This coalition will put a very strong force on your list of supporting factors.

Smart Web Performance Measurement

When I first started working with websites in the mid-1990s, I used to get a monthly stack of paper reports from our rudimentary analytics package, listing top visited pages, where our inbound traffic was coming from, and how many total files were served.

Tons of data, almost all of it useless. Page views went up 5 percent! Great! So what? Not much you can do with that knowledge.

Smart web performance measurement skips right past the high-level statistics and delves into the nitty-gritty of tracking specific actions or events on the site that indicate value has been delivered or created.

When Amazon.com was first founded they used to have a bell in their warehouse that rang every time someone bought something on the site.

As you might guess the bell was short lived as sales took off but it is a great example of tying a measure to a meaningful and valuable event. Think of your own site. What actions or events happen on your site that should have the equivalent of a bell in your office attached to it?

A few of the more common events or actions for association websites include

- Completed e-commerce transactions (I personally love this one!);
- Shared content via a social media or other widget;
- Successful/Failed login ratio; and
- Letter or email successfully sent to congressional representatives.

The list is potentially endless. The most important consideration is to identify what specific events or actions on your site show progress toward your most important goals.

Once you have the measures in place you now have a powerful tool for tracking improvement. You can experiment with small shifts in interface and design and see what makes the bell ring more often and what tends to silence it.

All performance measurement starts in one place. Identify what event demonstrates the most value creation on your site and figure out how to measure it. Once the measure is in place, work on improving that one metric. Dedicate yourself to it with maniacal focus. I once worked in a bookstore and to keep myself amused I used to pick a single title that I would try to sell out during my shift. Do the same thing here, pick a metric and see how far you can take it.

Forget everything else. Really, total page views matters not a whit unless you make most of your revenue from display advertising. You almost certainly don't, so move on. One solid measure that enables you to act to improve performance is worth more than all the traffic reports in the world and fancy dashboards.

Micro Web Strategy

Web strategy as defined and described in this book can be applied for very focused projects and outcomes in addition to the more comprehensive strategy projects. You can do this on your own for any project or work with a small team.

For example, if you are launching a new workshop, go through the process of identifying outcomes and audiences and pick one or two of the seven strategies that will best support your scenario. Jot down some notes on content, design, and functionality and you are off and running!

Website directors and managers can use this process as a template for consulting with other units in the organization, advising them how to achieve results online that contribute to their goals. Sometimes you have to push back on the preconceived ideas about what they *want to do* online and get them to focus on what they *need to achieve* online. Get the "what" defined first and then advise them on the best options for "how." Often you will get requests for new buttons or navigational links but you have no idea what outcomes they are actually trying to create. Dig deeper to identify the need behind the request and apply your knowledge, skills, and technology to best solve the problem or leverage an opportunity. Maybe they need a button, maybe they don't. You won't know until you get at the root of the issue.

Be Nimble

Don't turn your strategy into a straightjacket. The world is constantly changing around us as do the priorities of our organizations. As you build and refine your online presence look to how you can make it flexible enough to be quickly shifted to new needs and priorities. The two cases that follow, one of which is a 'what if' exercise and the other a nice example of responding to the flu crisis of 2009 without wrecking a home page, are useful for considering the nimbleness of your own web operations.

Case Study: Flu Crisis Response

In the spring of 2009, many organizations were grappling with how to respond to the emergent issue of the H1N1 Flu or Swine Flu that was spreading from Mexico. As of this writing, the immediate risk appears to have waned. However, health organizations in particular had to quickly ramp up their communications when the crisis first broke. The Massachusetts Medical Society (MMS) website provides an excellent example of rapid and flexible response.

MMS recently redesigned their site and have a feature position on the home page that can easily be dedicated to specific topics. Frank Fortin, who leads the web team at MMS, had his team create a custom graphic that leads to a clearinghouse of information on the flu for members and patients.

There are three things that enable MMS or any organization to use their home page flexibly and quickly like this.

Process: They have a defined management process in place for identifying emergent issues and how to decide when they should be featured. This doesn't have to be very formal or detailed but you do need to know who has to be part of the discussion and who will make the call.

People: Not only do you need to know who the decision maker is and have access to that person, you also need to know what technical or design talent you will need in such a case and how you will access them. Who will you use to design the graphic and how quickly can you access them and get something done? This is more critical when you rely on outside vendors for your web design.

Technology: Your web template must make it easy to pop in a feature like MMS did for their home page. Your content management system should also make it easy to put this kind of alert into place.

If you don't have a handle on those three factors in advance and how they relate to crisis communication you'll be behind the news on your home page just when everyone expects you to be out front.

Case Exercise:
Web Strategy Implications of an Open Cuba

Is your website ready for an open Cuba?

Remarks by the Presidents of Cuba and the United States in April of 2009 showed the first substantive cracks in a half-century standoff between the two countries. Cuba very well may open for trade and travel with the United States in the not too distant future. If it does, the web may be your association's first and best opportunity to engage within the Caribbean country.

Raul Castro, president of Cuba, set off the diplomatic reverberations when he stated in April that his country is open to discussing "everything" with its neighbor to the north. President Obama responded in kind by welcoming talks and changes in Cuba's policies. Of course, Fidel Castro threw some cold water on the issue when he later issued a statement repudiating his brother's comments. Nonetheless, Secretary of State Hilary Clinton pointed out that this shows the beginning of a debate within Cuba, the first to have ever spilled into the public.

Impact of an Open Cuba

I spoke with Alan Weiss, a world-renowned business consultant and author, about what opportunities an open Cuba might have for businesses, industry, and education. Weiss, president of Summit Consulting and former Vice President of Latin America and Asia for Kepner-Tregoe, said that "tourism, medical, entertainment, education, [and] small business consulting" are all areas to watch for significant opportunity and growth if trade between the United States and Cuba becomes a reality. When I asked about the likely importance of education and knowledge transfer for a newly open Cuba, Weiss responded, "Very high. I'm not underestimating their educational system, but the access to greater resources and freer thought would be enormous. Think of what their already fine medical training would profit with greater access and resources."

Associations can and should have a major role in all of those likely trends. Education and knowledge transfer are typically core strengths for many organizations. Regional groups focused on Latin America, North America, or even just Florida will likely have significant shifts and changes in their markets if trade and travel open between the two countries.

Serving new constituencies in Cuba is likely to be challenging. The web and other internet-based services may be a key channel for early efforts as well as a prime delivery platform as strategies and projects mature. However, some characteristics of Cuba's telecom infrastructure are likely to impose limitations on what can be done online at first.

Infrastructure and Audiences

According to *The World Factbook*, Cuba's telecom infrastructure woefully lags the rest of the Caribbean region. Cuba has about 10 fixed telephone lines per 100 inhabitants and only about 200,000 cell phones for a total population of over 11 million people. Internet access is tightly controlled by the government and not available to the general Cuban public except via black market passwords.

Given that, why would the web be a key avenue for serving and communicating within Cuba? Some trends in other developing countries show that access may spread much quicker than you might expect once Cuba begins to open.

First, if trade and travel liberalize, then control of internet access won't be far behind. At worst, the government will filter access to politically charged content as China does for their population. That will still leave Cuba with a woefully inadequate telecom infrastructure.

Countries such as India, the Philippines, and Vietnam rapidly built out wireless networks with cell phones becoming critical communication tools and drivers of development throughout the population. The same could happen for Cuba. In fact, President Obama's loosening of some restrictions on Cuba earlier this year included allowing more telecom investment in Cuba by U.S. companies.

If Cuba follows this pattern of development, the likely access point to the internet for a large part of the population will be via cellular phones and other mobile devices. These devices will also have to be very inexpensive or subsidized since current per capita GDP is less than $10,000. Income levels will surely grow if Cuba opens to trade, but that will take time.

There is also likely to be limited bandwidth available to internet-enabled devices as the network is built out. Cuba does not have a fiber-optic line to the island yet, so there may be significant choke points for internet traffic to and from the island as adoption grows.

The good news for internet adoption is that Cuba has a very high level of education, with almost 100 percent literacy. Once the country is networked to the globe-spanning internet, that medium will be the most efficacious way for Cubans to explore the rest of the world.

Potential Goals and Web Strategies

Every web strategy depends upon two things: the outcomes you wish to achieve and the people with whom you can achieve them. The web outcomes must serve higher-level goals of the organization. Your website audiences for those outcomes are typically derived from the markets that your organization serves.

In this case of Cuba, we are looking at a potential expansion of your markets to include people and organizations within the country as well as potential changes to your existing markets as they adapt and respond to such a big shift. Initially, I anticipate that most associations will not be focused on generating revenue from Cuba, but will take actions that support their overall mission and existing membership as it relates to Cuba. Therefore, a lot of early activities may focus on building awareness and serving the needs of people in Cuba congruent with the organization's mission. Establishing these initial relationships will position the association to have many opportunities to better serve these constituents in the future.

Let's take medicine as an example. Cuba is often cited as having an advanced medical field, supplying doctors to countries throughout Latin America. Associations that represent medical technology or supply companies might focus on raising awareness of the value their members' products and services could provide to the Cuban medical community. Likewise, medical specialty associations will need to conduct outreach and education about the value of their organization and publications and begin to build direct relationships with their colleagues in Cuba.

Both of these examples have goals that could be served by a market needs-focused web strategy. In this strategy, the organization determines the content, design, and functionality of their website based on what would best serve the needs of a specific audience. Providing content, education, and collaboration opportunities online for the Cuban medical community as they begin to engage with colleagues in North America is a highly focused strategy that can be used to guide implementation online.

Given the state of telecommunications in Cuba and the likely growth of wireless as a primary vehicle for going online, these hypothetical associations should focus on creating websites that deploy content and services using techniques and technology that are very mobile friendly and usable even with low bandwidth.

This approach leads to website design that is very light on graphics and rich media such as video or even Flash. Sites will have to be focused on text supported with only the graphics needed to illustrate specific concepts. The content presentation and navigation must accommodate the small screen in order to be effective for this audience. Text messaging and social media tools such as Twitter may also be likely platforms for early engagement.

In summary, initial online efforts for a newly open Cuba must be of high value to your desired audiences while accommodating the likely bandwidth limitations and mobile-centric browsers and technology.

Looking Forward with the Web

I grant that this discussion of an open Cuba is largely a thought experiment at this stage. However, if the past year has taught us anything, it is that change can be rapid and lead to highly unexpected events and results. Those who pay attention to the early trends are able to respond effectively. The same is true for Cuba.

Someday there will be trade between our two countries and the internet will be a key platform for engagement. Will you be ready?

Case Exercise

After reading the case above, consider the following questions and tasks. You may do these by yourself or, more interestingly, use them as a brainstorming exercise for a team or leadership meeting.

- If Cuba opens up, whom would you want to reach in the country? To what end?

- What priorities would your members have vis-à-vis Cuba?

- Given the above, what would be your initial outcomes online and the specific audiences you wish to address?

- Draft a web strategy profile based on the above. What would this entail for the content, design, and functionality of your site?

- How might heavy adoption of cellular devices for internet access change your approach to serving audiences in Cuba?

Your Breakthrough Results

The one thing I hope you take away from this book, if nothing else, is that our online work must be focused on making tangible contributions to the top priorities of our organizations. Any website can benefit from this kind of focus. All organizations can take their results to new heights if their web presence becomes a significant contributor to their goals.

Breakthrough results can be large or small, qualitative or quantitative. The important thing is that you are acting with intent to create these outcomes online after considering the bigger picture of your top-level mission and strategy. Throughout the book I have shared examples of breakthrough results. These included:

- Hearst used their online presence to drive print subscriptions to their magazines and purposely did not use online advertising revenue as their driving force;

- The Ecological Society of America tailored their design and content to emphasize the emotional bond that ecologists have with their science and the organization;

- The Air Conditional Contractors of America shifted a series of one-off webinars into a subscription service, making them easier to market and increasing overall revenue; and

- The Massachusetts Medical Society used their home page to facilitate an emergency next action of driving visitors to critical information about the H1N1 influenza outbreak of early 2009.

In each case, the organization used the web as an effective means to important ends for their organization, volunteers, members, and ultimately, their mission. They embody being online and on mission.

Each of us, from the board member to the solo webmaster to technology vendors and web designers has the potential to make a real and substantial difference in the mission of our organizations. I hope that some of the ideas, tools, and processes in this book will aid you in realizing that potential. We are all doing good work and serving excellent causes. Go forth and achieve breakthrough results for your mission today!

assign roles
clearly defined